The MAILBOX®

The Education Center®

grade **1**

MATH INDEPENDENT PRACTICE

SUPER SIMPLE!

EASY-TO-USE IDEAS FOR SKILL REINFORCEMENT

- ☑ Addition
- ☑ Subtraction
- ☑ Number sense
- ☑ Patterns
- ☑ Money
- ☑ Geometry
- ☑ Word problems
- ☑ **AND LOTS MORE!**

ENOUGH FOR

4 activities for every w... OF THE SCHOOL YEAR

D1402588

Managing Editor: Lynn Drolet

Editorial Team: Becky S. Andrews, Randi Austin, Diane Badden, Cindy Barber, Amy Barsanti, Kimberley Bruck, Karen A. Brudnak, Kitty Campbell, Jenny Chapman, LeeAnn Collins, Pam Crane, Chris Curry, Stacie Stone Davis, Lynette Dickerson, Deborah Garmon, Mary Ann Gildroy, Theresa Lewis Goode, Tazmen Hansen, Marsha Heim, Lori Z. Henry, Lori Henson, Shelley Hoster, Cynthia Holcomb, Sherry Hull, Debra Liverman, Beth Marquardt, Dorothy C. McKinney, Thad H. McLaurin, Lisa Mountcasel, Sharon Murphy, Jennifer Nunn, Doris Porter, Gerri Primak, Mark Rainey, Greg D. Rieves, Janet Robbins, Mary Robles, Hope Rodgers, Eliseo De Jesus Santos II, Rebecca Saunders, Carol Schott, Betty Silkunas, Andrea M. Singleton, Joshua Thomas, Stephanie Turner, Carole Watkins, Zane Williard

www.themailbox.com

©2008 The Mailbox® Books
All rights reserved.
ISBN10 #1-56234-845-0 • ISBN13 #978-156234-845-8

Manufactured in the United States
10 9 8 7 6 5 4 3 2 1

Table of Contents

To use the table of contents as a checklist, make a copy of pages 2 and 3. Staple or clip each copy on top of its original page. Each time you use an activity, check its box. Start each school year with fresh copies of the pages.

Skills Index on pages 111-112.

Show the Number

Counting

Materials:
tagboard number tracers 1–9
bingo daubers, stampers, or small stickers
blank paper

A student traces a number on his paper. He uses the bingo dauber, stickers, or stampers to place the corresponding number of dots or objects on the number. He repeats the steps with each remaining number as time permits.

A Fine Assortment

Sorting

Materials:
cutouts of different colors and sizes

A student sorts the cutouts by color and then sorts the collection again by size. For an added challenge, she sorts the cutouts using both attributes at once.

Make 'em Match!

Counting

Materials:
cups numbered 1–10
tub of counters

A child takes a cup, reads the number, and puts the corresponding number of counters inside. She repeats the process for each of the remaining nine cups. For an added challenge, she puts the cups in numerical order.

Bean Bonanza

Graphing

Materials:
student copies of page 76, programmed with title
tub of various dried beans
small scoop
crayons
glue

A student glues a different bean at the bottom of each column. Then he gets a scoopful of beans and glues each bean in the corresponding column. He outlines the resulting towers to complete the graph.

Kinds of Beans

10					
9					
8					
7			○		
6	○		○		
5	○		○		
4	○	○	○	○	
3	○	○	○	○	○
2	○	○	○	○	○
1	○	○	○	○	○
	○	○	○	○	○

Domino Designs

Equivalent sets

Materials:
dominoes
blank paper
crayons

A student counts the dots on a domino and creates a matching paper domino, replacing each dot set with an equal set of drawings of another object. She continues in this manner, making more dominoes, as time permits. For an added challenge, she writes the corresponding number for each set.

Helpful Chains

Comparing numbers

Materials:
tub of math links
scoop
blank paper

A student gets a scoopful of math links and uses the links to make a chain. She counts the links and writes the number on her paper. Then she gets a second scoopful of links and repeats each step. Next, she compares the two numbers she wrote and circles the larger one. To continue, she unlinks each chain, returns the links to the tub, and begins a new round.

Pom-Poms to Polka Dots!

Equivalent sums

Materials:
student copies of page 77
bag of small pom-poms of two colors
scissors
crayons

A student cuts out the hat and writes a specified sum at the top. He places the corresponding number of pom-poms on the top of the hat. Then he draws matching-colored dots on the top row and returns the pom-poms to the bag. He removes the same number of pom-poms and draws to show equivalent forms of the same sum. He continues in this manner for each remaining row.

That Pesky Fly!

Positional words

Materials:
student copies of the fly and word cards
    on page 78
magazines
blank paper
scissors
glue

A student cuts out a set of cards and four magazine pictures. He glues the pictures on his paper and then glues a word card below each one. To show his understanding of each word or phrase, he glues a fly card in the corresponding position.

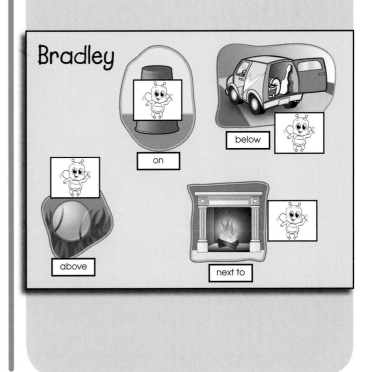

Up and Down

Addition sentences to 7

Materials:
bag with 7 plastic bottle caps
lined paper

A student shakes the bag, empties the contents, and draws pictures to show how many caps landed faceup and how many caps landed facedown. Then she writes the corresponding number sentence. She continues in this manner as time permits.

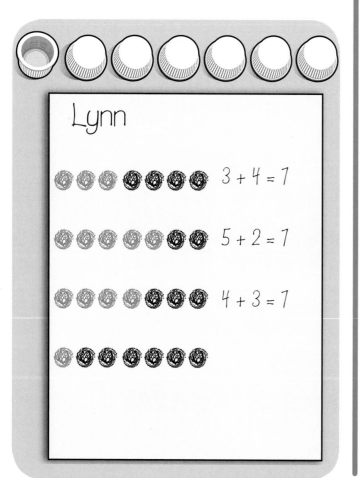

Keep It Going

Patterns

Materials:
cards programmed with patterns like
    the ones shown
pattern blocks
paper strips
crayons

A child selects a card and places pattern blocks on a blank strip to match the pattern. Then she extends the pattern to the end of the strip. Next, she traces the blocks and colors them to show the pattern.

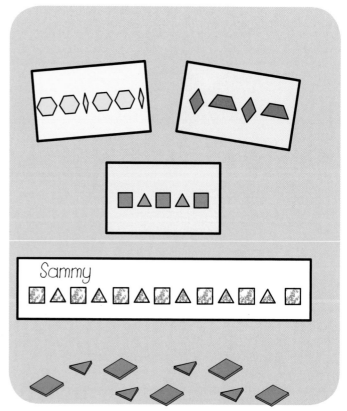

Decorative Dates

Calendar

Materials:
current month's calendar
blank calendar (one per student)
crayons

To understand the parts of a calendar, a student refers to the programmed calendar to write the name of the month, days of the week, and dates on the blank calendar. Then he embellishes the calendar with drawings to mark special dates.

All in Order

Ordering numbers

Materials:
bag of numbered cards 0–20
lined paper

A youngster removes five cards from the bag, places them faceup, and orders the numbers from least to greatest. He copies the numbers on a sheet of paper and returns the cards to the bag. Then he shakes the bag and begins again.

Roll and Write

Positional words

Materials:
cube programmed with positional words
blank paper
crayons

A youngster makes a self-portrait in the center of his paper. Then he rolls the cube and reads the word. He draws an object on his paper in the corresponding location and labels it with the positional word. He continues to roll and write as time permits.

George
← on
← under

over
beside   under

Schools of Fish

Sums to 12

Materials:
playing cards (aces to 6)
light blue paper (one per student)
crayons

A student takes a card and uses one color to draw the corresponding number of fish on a sheet of paper. Then she takes another card and uses a different color to draw the fish. Next, she writes a number sentence to describe her school of fish. To continue, she turns her paper over and repeats each step.

$$6 + 3 = 9$$

Color Towers

Graphing

Materials:
student copies of page 76
supply of counters (five different colors)
crayons

A child labels a copy of the grid with different-colored circles to match the counter colors. Then she takes a handful of counters and colors the boxes to show how many she has of each color. For an added challenge, she writes a sentence or two about her resulting graph.

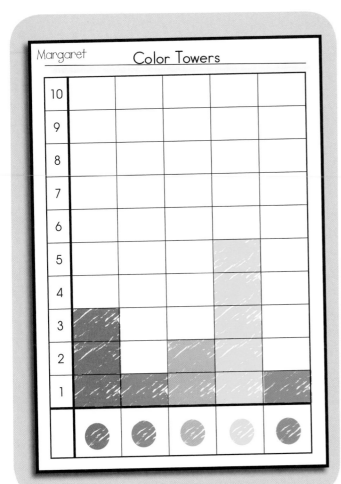

Cool Caterpillar!

Counting by 10s

Materials:
student copies of page 79
construction paper (one per student)
scissors
crayons
glue

A child cuts out the caterpillar head and circle patterns. He arranges them on the construction paper behind the head cutout to show counting by tens. Then he glues them in place to make a caterpillar. If time permits, he adds details.

Prickly Porcupine

Addition

Materials:
addition flash cards
large ball of clay or play dough
2 wiggle eyes
toothpicks
blank paper

A student forms his clay into a simple porcupine shape and adds two wiggle eyes. He draws a card and inserts toothpicks (quills) into the clay to model the addition problem. He copies the problem on his paper and writes the answer. He then removes the toothpicks and repeats with the remaining cards.

Animals on Parade

Ordinal numbers

Materials:
10 small stuffed toy animals
cards labeled with ordinal numbers 1st through 10th

A child puts ten stuffed animals in a line, one in front of the other, as if they were in a parade. She places each ordinal number card beside the corresponding animal.

How Many?

Estimation

Materials:
resealable plastic bag containing fewer than 50 counters
10 additional counters in a second color
blank paper

A youngster places the ten unbagged counters side by side at the top of his paper. Then, he examines the counters in the bag without opening it. Next, using the unbagged counters as a reference, he writes on his paper an estimate of how many counters are in the bag. He then opens the bag, counts the contents, and records the actual number.

Batch of Cookies

Patterns

Materials:
student copies of the cookie cards on page 80
3" x 12" construction paper strips (one per student)
crayons
scissors
glue

A child colors each type of cookie the same way; then he cuts out the cards. Next, he uses the cards to form a pattern of his choosing. Once he has checked his pattern, he glues the cards in place on the strip, discarding cards he didn't use. For an added challenge, the student writes the type of pattern (*AB*, *ABB*, or *AAB*) on the back of his strip.

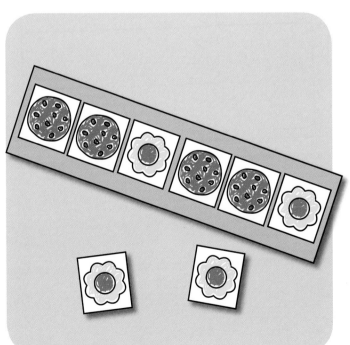

Batter Up!

Ordering numbers

Materials:
copy of the baseball bat cards on page 81, cut
    out and labeled with different numbers
student copies of the recording sheet on page 81

A youngster takes a bat cutout and copies the number on her recording sheet. Then she writes the next three numbers in order in each baseball. She continues in this manner until she has completed her sheet. For an added challenge, the child turns her paper over and writes three more number sequences.

Crazy Face

Plane shapes

Materials:
student copies of the recording sheet on page 80
several construction paper cutouts of
    each of the following shapes in
    various sizes and colors: circle,
    triangle, square, rectangle
yarn
blank paper
crayons
glue

A student uses the shapes to create a face on his paper and then glues the shape in place. He counts the number of each type of shape he used and writes the totals on his recording sheet. He then adds details with crayons and yarn. For an added challenge, the child writes a sentence about the crazy face at the bottom of his recording sheet.

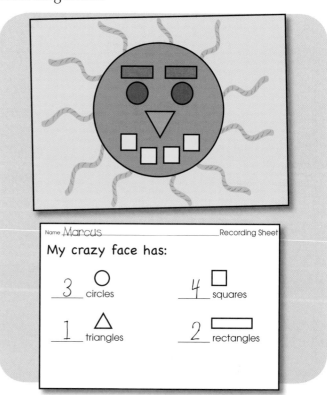

Domino Rubbings

Addition

Materials:
dominoes
blank paper
crayons

A youngster folds his paper in half three times and then unfolds it to make eight sections. He selects a domino and places it under the first section. He then colors over the domino to make a rubbing. Below the rubbing, he writes the corresponding number sentence. He repeats this process with seven other dominoes until each section is filled.

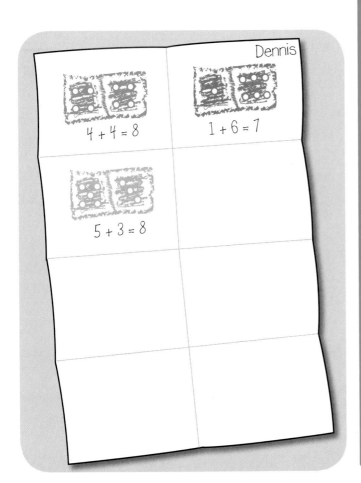

String Things

Nonstandard measurement

Materials:
length of yarn taped to a tabletop
objects of varying sizes
blank paper

A student folds her paper in half, unfolds it, and labels each section as shown. For each object, she predicts whether it is longer or shorter than the yarn length. Next, she measures each object against the yarn length to check her prediction. Then she lists or draws each object in the corresponding section of her paper.

Flower Power

Addition

Materials:
student copies of page 82, programmed
    with addition problems
ink pads in two different colors

A student chooses a color of ink and makes fingerprint petals around her first flower to match the first addend. She uses a different color to make petals to match the second addend. She counts the petals to solve the problem and records her answer on the leaf. She repeats the steps with the remaining problems. For an added challenge, the child cuts out the flowers, orders the sums from least to greatest, and glues the flowers on a paper strip.

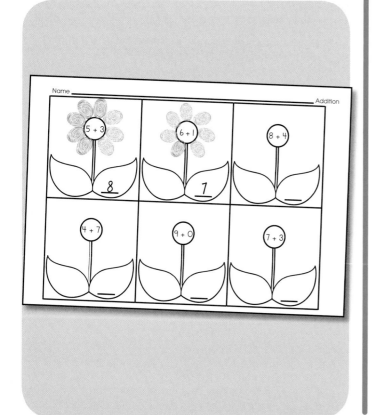

Calendar Cut Up

Ordering numbers

Materials:
2 copies of the same calendar month, one
    of which is cut into numbered squares

A child shuffles the squares and then places them in numerical order. When she is finished, she uses the other calendar to check her work.

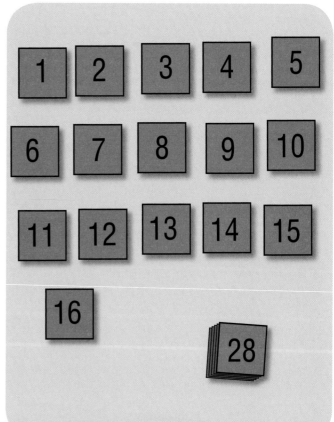

In the Bag

Patterns

Materials:
bag with pairs of different objects
blank paper
crayons

Possible objects include Unifix cubes, pattern blocks, counters, paper clips, and erasers.

A student randomly selects three objects from the bag and places them in a row to form the beginning of a pattern. He draws the three objects on his paper and extends the pattern. Then he returns the items to the bag and repeats the process to make different patterns.

Get Cracking!

Building sets

Materials:
8 or more plastic eggs, each containing a numbered paper strip
basket to hold the eggs
blank paper

A student folds her paper in half three times and then unfolds it to create eight sections. She opens an egg, reads the number on the strip, and writes it in a section of her paper. Next, she draws a corresponding number of items in the section. Then she returns the strip to the egg and continues with different eggs for the remaining sections on her paper.

Set 8

Picture This

Graphing

Materials:
two-column bar graph (one per student)
magazines
blank paper
scissors
glue

> Possible category pairs include plants/animals, cars/trucks, happy/sad, and indoor things/outdoor things.

A child chooses a category pair and copies the labels onto his graph. Next, he cuts out magazine pictures that match the categories on his graph and glues each one in its corresponding section. Then, on another sheet of paper, he writes two sentences that tell about his graph.

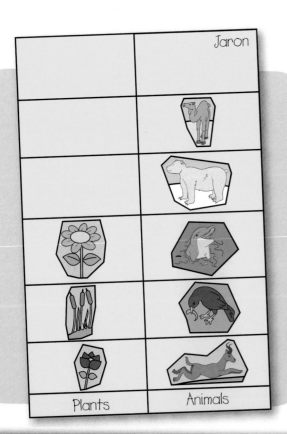

Stick to It!

Addition

Materials:
several disposable cups, each containing
    up to 15 paper clips of two different colors
    (vary the quantities in each cup)
magnetic wand
blank paper

A student uses the magnet to remove several paper clips from one cup. She sorts them by color. Then she writes two addition sentences on her paper based on the paper clips. She returns the paper clips to the cup and repeats the process with the remaining cups.

Maria

1. $6 + 3 = 9$
   $3 + 6 = 9$
2. $5 + 7 = 12$
   $7 + 5 = 12$

Sides and Corners

Plane shapes

Materials:
straws cut in various lengths
clay or play dough
circle template
construction paper (one per student)
clear tape

A youngster uses the straws and clay to make a triangle, a rectangle, and a square. She tapes each shape to her paper as she completes it. Then she traces the circle template on her paper. She labels each shape with its name. For an added challenge, the student writes the number of sides and corners of each shape.

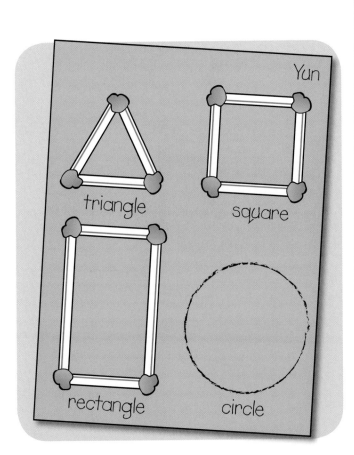

Fill It In

Ordering numbers to 50

Materials:
copies of page 83 (one grid per student)

A student writes the missing numbers on the grid. For an added challenge, he uses a crayon to shade all the even-numbered boxes.

Set 9

Super Stamping

Sets to 100

Materials:
stampers
ink pad
hundreds board
pom-pom
1" graph paper

A student tosses a pom-pom onto the hundreds board and identifies the number on which it lands. She writes the number on her paper and uses the stamps to make a corresponding set of objects. She continues in this manner as time permits.

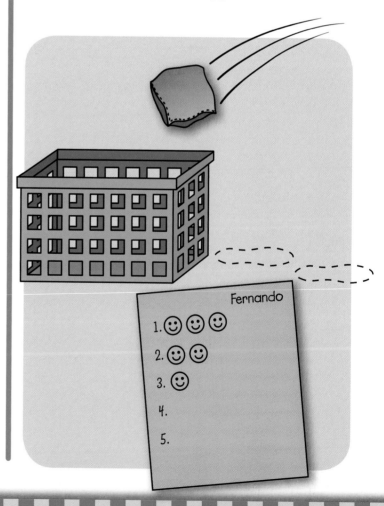

Score!

Collecting data

Materials:
large basket
beanbag
blank paper

A youngster numbers his paper from one to five. For each number, he takes the corresponding number of steps away from the basket and tries to toss the beanbag into the basket three times. For each successful toss, he draws a smiley face next to the corresponding number on his paper. For an added challenge, he uses the data to write sentences that tell from how many paces away he was most and least successful.

Super Simple Independent Practice: Math • ©The Mailbox® Books • TEC61154

Hoop Hop

Probability

Materials:
plastic hoop
bag of 24 red counters
1 yellow counter

A child puts the yellow counter in with the bag of red counters and shakes the bag. She removes one counter without looking at it, predicts its color, and looks at it to confirm if she is correct. If correct, she hops in and out of the plastic hoop. She continues in this manner to discover red will be the most likely color!

Leaping Lily Pads!

Counting by 5s

Materials:
student copies of page 84
skip-counting pattern
scissors

A student writes the numbers in the skip-counting pattern on the lily pad cards. He cuts out the cards and puts them in order. Then he cuts out the frog pattern of his choice, folds it, and chants the skip-counting pattern as he moves the frog from card to card. For an added challenge, provide extra copies of the lily pad cards for youngsters to continue the pattern to 100.

5, 10, 15, 20, 25, 30, 35, 40, 45, 50

5 10 15 20 35 30 25 40 45 50

Double Dip

Doubles addition

Materials:
triangle cutouts (ten per student)
strip numbered from 1–10
12" x 18" blank paper
crayons
glue

A student folds his paper lengthwise and unfolds it. He glues ten triangles (cones) on his paper, as shown, and draws two ice cream scoops atop each cone. Then he uses the numbers on the strip to write a different doubles addition problem on each ice cream treat.

How Many Corners?

Plane shapes

Materials:
shapes, one of each shown
blank paper
crayons

A student folds her paper to make four boxes; unfolds it; and, using the numbers 0, 3, 4, and 6, labels each box with a different number. Then she looks at each shape, counts any corners it may have, and draws or traces the shape in the corresponding box. For an added challenge, she labels each shape.

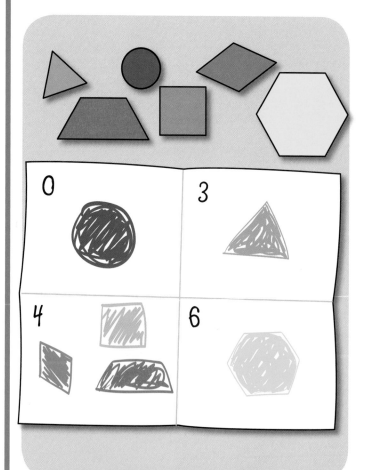

Picnic Pals

Fractions

Materials:
blank paper
crayons

A student draws five different picnic treats on her paper. Then she draws a line to show how she could divide each treat to share it equally with a friend.

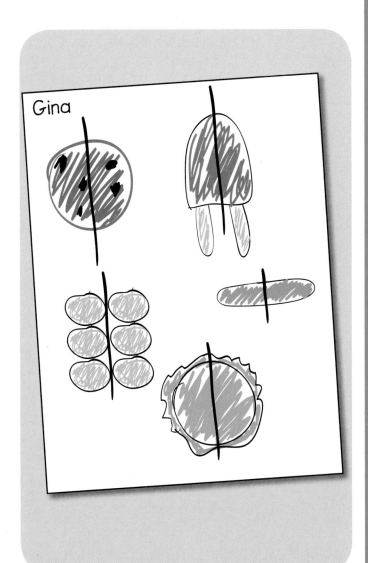

Pigs in the Mud

Addition word problems

Materials:
student copies of page 85
brown construction paper shape (mud hole)
blank paper
scissors
glue

A student cuts out the word problem and pig cards. He takes a word problem card, glues it to his paper, and uses the pig cards and the mud hole to help him solve the problem. Then he writes the answer next to the card. He continues in this manner with each remaining word problem card.

Geometric Rainbow

Plane shapes

Materials:
student copies of the shape workmat on page 86
picture of a rainbow (color reference)
large blank paper (one per student)
6 crayons (red, yellow, orange, green, blue, purple)

A student draws seven arcs on her blank paper to make the color outlines of a rainbow. Next, she identifies each shape on her workmat and then colors each shape a different color. Then she uses the rainbow reference to draw the corresponding colored shape in each arc on her paper.

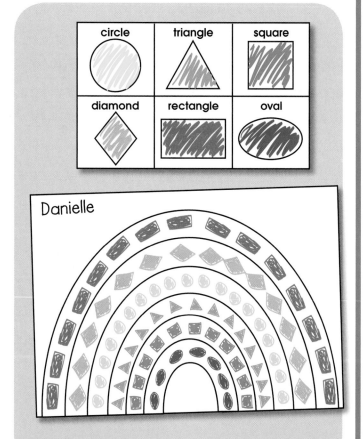

A Valuable Collection

Sorting coins

Materials:
copy of the coin cards on page 78, cut out
supply of coins

A youngster reads the name of the coin pictured on each card. Then he sorts the coins into four corresponding piles. For an added challenge, he counts each pile of money and records the total value of each coin set.

On a Roll

Commutative property of addition

Materials:
pair of dice
smiley-face stickers or crayons
writing paper

A student rolls the dice and uses the numbers to write an addition sentence. Then he switches the order of the numbers rolled to write a second addition sentence. He continues in this manner for each roll of the dice. If a double is rolled, he writes one addition sentence and places or draws a smiley face on his paper!

Cube Count!

Nonstandard measurement

Materials:
student copies of page 87
Unifix cubes
writing paper
crayons: blue and yellow

A student writes the letters *A* through *H* on her writing paper. Then she uses the cubes to measure each bug and records its height and length next to the corresponding letters. To complete the activity, have her follow the directions to color by the code.

Build a Pyramid

Equivalent sums

Materials:
copy of the pyramid workmat on page 88
supply of dominoes (dot sums from 3 to 12)
blank paper

A student counts the number of dots on a domino and places the domino on the corresponding number on the workmat. He continues in this manner with the remaining dominoes, stacking dominoes with equivalent sums. Then he selects a stack and, using each domino's dots, writes number sentences for that sum.

Connor

$4 + 2 = 6$

$6 + 0 = 6$

$3 + 3 = 6$

Subtraction Stampede

Writing subtraction sentences

Materials:
red number cards from 1–5
green number cards from 6–10
ink pad
stamper
blank paper

A student takes a green card and makes the corresponding number of stamps on her paper. Then she takes a red card and crosses out the corresponding number of stamps. Next, she uses the illustration to write a subtraction sentence. She continues in this manner with the remaining cards.

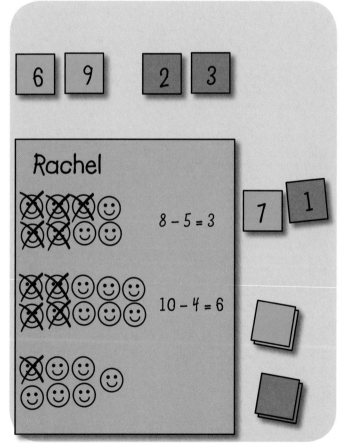

Rachel

$8 - 5 = 3$

$10 - 4 = 6$

Goody Goody Gumballs

Graphing

Materials:
student copies of page 76 titled as shown
student copies of page 89
5 crayons of different colors

A student uses five different colors of crayons to color the gumballs on page 89. Then he labels the bottom of his graph with gumballs in matching colors. Next, he creates a graph to show how many gumballs of each color are in his gumball machine.

A First-Grade Lineup!

Ordinal numbers

Materials:
student copies of the recording sheet on page 88
crayons

A student labels each letter in the words *First Grade* with the corresponding ordinal number. Then she follows the directions as written on the workmat to color each of the letters.

First Grade — Mariah

1st 2nd 3rd 4th 5th   6th 7th 8th 9th 10th

A. Color the **2nd** letter orange.
B. Color the **7th** letter yellow.
C. Color the **1st** letter red.
D. Color the **8th** letter blue.
E. Color the **3rd** letter yellow.

F. Color the **5th** letter brown.
G. Color the **9th** letter purple.
H. Color the **4th** letter green.
I. Color the **10th** letter black.
J. Color the **6th** letter red.

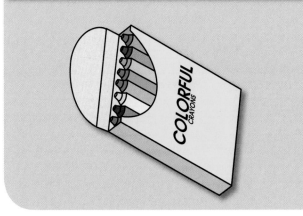

Cutups

Counting by 10s and 5s

Materials:
laminated hundred chart (or paper copy of a
   hundred chart for each student)
sentence strips
wipe-off marker (or crayon if paper copy is provided)
damp paper towel
scissors

A student draws a line around each box on
the hundred chart containing a number used in
counting by tens. She then uses the chart as a
guide as she writes each highlighted number on
a sentence strip. She then cuts the numbers apart,
places them in a stack, and erases her chart with
the paper towel. She repeats this process, this
time counting by fives, until she has two stacks
of cards. She shuffles a stack, puts the cards in
order, and repeats with the other stack of cards.

Riddle Me This

Plane shapes

Materials:
pattern blocks
blank paper
crayons

A youngster selects a shape to describe. He
folds his paper in half. On the front, he writes a
riddle about his shape as shown. Inside, he draws
his shape and writes the answer to the riddle.

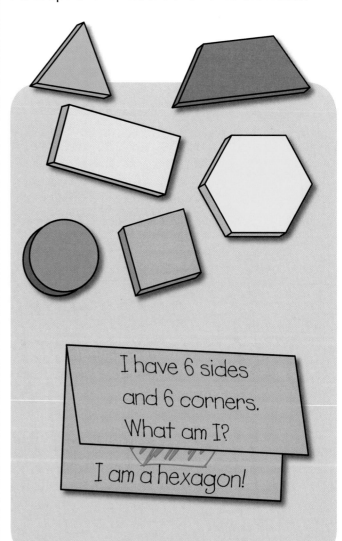

I have 6 sides
and 6 corners.
What am I?

I am a hexagon!

Flower Seeds

Subtraction to 12

Materials:
copy of the sunflower workmat on page 86
subtraction flash cards
10 construction paper seed cutouts
blank paper

A child chooses a card and copies the problem onto his paper. Then he uses the seed cutouts and the workmat to help him solve the problem and writes the answer on his paper. He repeats the activity with different flash cards as time allows.

Call It a Day

Time

Materials:
magazines
sheet of white construction paper (one per student)
blank clock stamper
ink pad
scissors
glue

A student cuts out a magazine picture of a morning activity and another of a night activity. Next, she folds her construction paper in half, unfolds it, and stamps a blank clock at the top of each section. She glues one picture in each section and then draws clock hands to represent the hour closest to when each pictured activity would take place. To complete the activity, she writes the digital time with AM or PM beside each clock.

Ice Cube Computation

Addition to 18

Materials:
plastic ice cube tray, labeled with numbers
two small pom-poms
blank paper

A child randomly drops each pom-pom into a different section. Then he writes the corresponding addition problem and answer on his paper. He continues in this manner until he has completed ten problems. For subtraction practice, the student turns his paper over and repeats the activity, this time subtracting the smaller number from the larger number and recording the problems.

Build It Yourself

Patterns

Materials:
blank cards programmed with patterns as shown
objects for patterning
blank paper
crayons

Possible objects include pattern blocks, beads, cubes, and counters

A child selects a card and uses the objects to create and extend the pattern shown on the card. Then she draws and labels the pattern on her paper. She continues in this manner with the remaining cards.

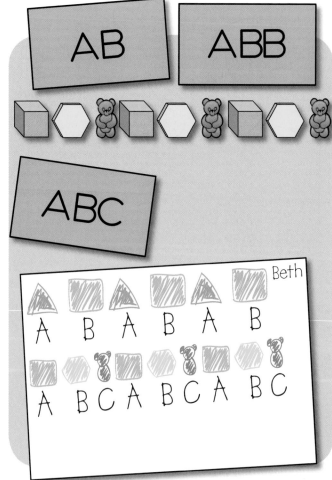

Tallyho!

Count and read numbers

Materials:
copy of the cards on page 90, cut apart

A youngster sorts the cards into two stacks. She shuffles each stack and places each card faceup. To play, she chooses a card with tally marks and counts to find the total. She then locates the matching number card to form a pair. She continues until she has paired up all the cards. For an added challenge, the student writes the numbers on a sheet of paper and draws tally marks to match.

Cans of Worms

Comparing numbers

Materials:
3 containers, labeled as shown
apple cutout labeled with a number
green paper strips (worms), each labeled with a different number

A student lays the worms facedown on a work surface. He turns over a worm and determines if the number is greater than, less than, or equal to the number on the apple. Then he places the worm in the corresponding container and repeats the process until all the worms have been sorted. For an added challenge, the child writes the number sentences on a sheet of paper.

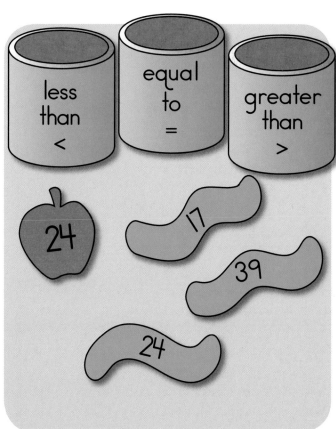

Set 15

What a Catch!

Subtraction

Materials:
cup containing 12 paper clips
weak magnet
blank paper

A student lowers the magnet into the cup of paper clips and then quickly pulls it out. He counts the paper clips on the magnet and uses them to write and solve a subtraction problem from 12. To check his answer, he counts the paper clips remaining in the cup. Then he returns the paper clips to the cup and repeats the activity as time allows.

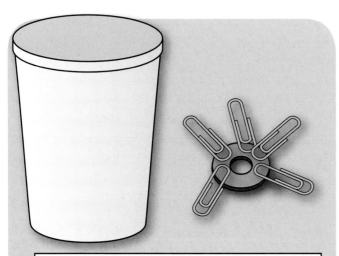

Jonathan

1. $12 - 3 = 9$
2. $12 - 8 = 4$
3. $12 - 5 = 7$

Sort Me!

Classify shapes

Materials:
shapes in a variety of colors, sizes, textures, and thicknesses
blank cards, each programmed with a different sorting rule
blank paper
crayons

Possible shapes include pattern blocks, foam shapes, or paper cutouts

A youngster takes a card and sorts the shapes according to the rule on the card. Next, she traces and colors the shapes on her paper and writes the sorting rule. Then she sorts the collection using a different rule. For an added challenge, the student writes her own rule and sorts the shapes using that rule.

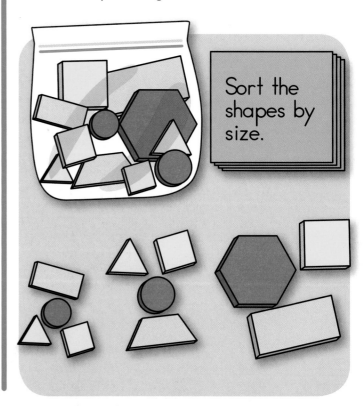

Sort the shapes by size.

Fair Shares

Fractions

Materials:
supply of die-cut shapes (six per student)
construction paper (one per student)
scissors
glue

A child labels a sheet of construction paper with the headings shown. She folds three die-cut shapes in half, being careful to line up the sides. She unfolds each shape and cuts it into two equal parts. Then she glues each shape in the "Equal Parts" column, leaving a space between the parts. Next, she folds the remaining shapes, this time not lining up the sides. Then she cuts each shape into two unequal parts and glues them in the "Unequal Parts" column.

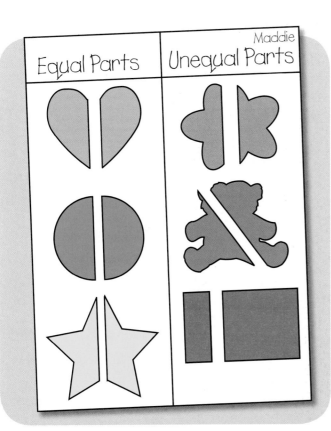

Fuzzy Lengths

Nonstandard measurement

Materials:
3 pipe cleaners (each a different color and length)
large object to measure with marked beginning and end points
blank paper

A student chooses a pipe cleaner and uses it to measure the object from beginning to end. After recording the measurement, he repeats the process with the remaining two pipe cleaners, recording his measurements each time. To conclude, he writes sentences explaining the results.

Set 16

Finish the Story

Addition word problems

Materials:
student copies of page 91
container of number tiles

A student randomly chooses two number tiles from the container. She places each tile on a blank in the first story problem on her paper. She reads the problem and writes the corresponding number sentence. She removes the tiles, takes two more, and repeats the activity to complete her paper.

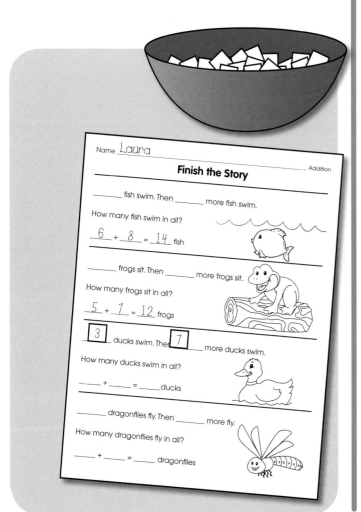

Let's Trade

Money

Materials:
cube labeled with numbers 1–6
supply of penny and nickel counters

A child rolls the cube, takes a corresponding number of pennies, and rolls again. When he has five pennies, he trades them for a nickel. He continues rolling, gathering pennies, and trading for nickels in this manner as time allows. For an added challenge, the student trades nickels for dimes.

Square Off

Subtraction to 12

Materials:
12 small construction paper squares
plastic cup
blank paper

A student holds all 12 paper squares above the cup and drops them. He counts how many squares fall in the cup and how many land outside. On his paper, he writes a number sentence to show how many squares are taken away (land in the cup) from the original 12 and how many are left (outside the cup). He repeats the activity as time allows.

Take a Spin!

Graphing

Materials:
copy of the spinner pattern and pet cards on page 92, prepared as shown
student copies of the graph on page 76, labeled with a title and the pet cards on page 92
crayons

A youngster spins the spinner and colors a cell in the matching column on her graph. She continues spinning and recording data until one of the columns is full. For an added challenge, the student writes a sentence on the back of her paper telling about her graph.

Ten Tens!

Addition combinations to 10

Materials:
playing cards (tens and face cards removed)
blank hundred chart (one per student)
lined paper
crayons

A student finds two or three cards whose values equal ten when added together. She uses different colors to shade the corresponding number of spaces for each card on the top row of her hundred chart. Then she writes the addition sentence on her paper. She continues in this manner for the remaining nine rows on the chart.

Ronda

$2 + 8 = 10$
$7 + 3 = 10$
$5 + 3 + 2 = 10$
$9 + 1 = 10$
$6 + 2 + 2 = 10$
$5 + 5 = 10$
$8 + 2 = 10$
$6 + 4 = 10$
$7 + 2 + 1 = 10$
$9 + 1 = 10$

Anyone Left Out?

Even and odd numbers

Materials:
supply of counters
scoop
blank paper

A youngster makes a T chart and writes the headers "even" and "odd." Then he empties a scoop of counters in his workspace and groups them in pairs. If all the counters have a partner, he writes the total number in the even column; if one is left out, he writes the total number in the odd column. He continues in this manner with more scoops as time permits.

Harry

Even	Odd
10	15
14	7
18	
12	

Undercover Exploration

Plane shapes

Materials:
paper bags labeled 1–4, each containing
  a different plastic, foam, or tagboard shape
blank paper

A student numbers his paper from 1 to 4. Then he reaches into each bag, without looking, and uses his sense of touch to determine what shape is in the bag. He writes his predictions next to the corresponding number on his paper. After looking into the bags to check his answers, he writes details about each shape as time permits. For an easier version, provide a copy of the shape cards on page 86 for students to use as a reference.

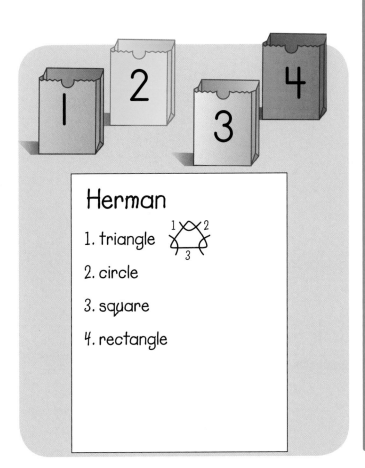

Herman

1. triangle
2. circle
3. square
4. rectangle

What's Next?

Number order

Materials:
number cards from 0 to 100
lined paper

A youngster takes two cards at random and writes the smaller number on her paper. Then she writes each subsequent number up to the number displayed on her other card. She continues in this manner as time permits.

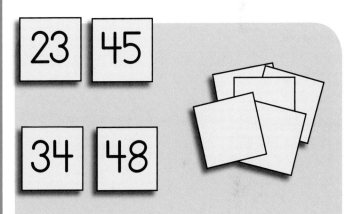

Yolanda

23, 24, 25, 26, 27, 28, 29, 30, 31,

32, 33, 34, 35, 36, 37, 38, 39, 40,

41, 42, 43, 44, 45

34, 35, 36, 37, 38, 39, 40, 41, 42,

43, 44, 45, 46, 47, 48

Set 18

Up, Up, and Away!

Addition to 18

Materials:
student copies of page 93
playing cards (tens and face cards removed)

A student adds the value of two cards and looks for the matching sum on his paper. Then he uses the card values as addends and completes the addition sentence. If the cards do not equal a sum on his paper, he continues to take more cards until a match is made. He reshuffles the cards as needed to complete each addition sentence.

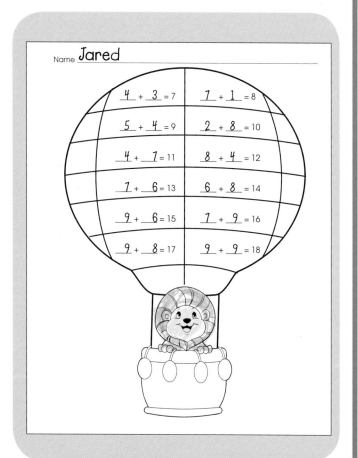

Footprint Fun

Nonstandard measurement

Materials:
lima beans
yarn lengths (equal in size)
paper squares (equal in size)
blank paper
crayons

A youngster traces around her foot on the left side of her blank paper. Then she arranges the beans, yarn, and squares to make three lines that are equal in length to her footprint and glues them in place. Then she counts the objects in each line and records the measurement.

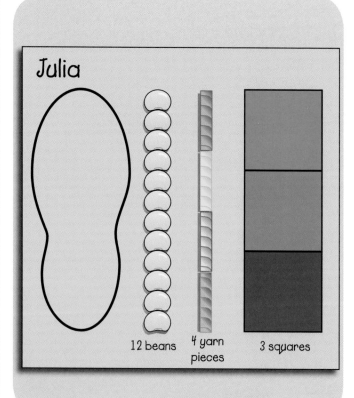

What a Wheel!

Subtraction to 18

Materials:
student copies of page 94
subtraction flash cards
brass fasteners (one per student)
blank paper
scissors

A student cuts out the patterns, places the arrow wheel on top of the number wheel, and secures the pieces with the fastener. Then he copies a flash card fact on his paper and uses the wheel to solve the problem. For an added challenge, combine addition flash cards with the subtraction cards for a mixed review.

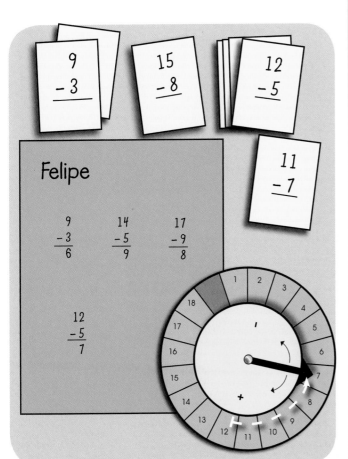

Organized Inventory

Tally marks

Materials:
collection of office materials
blank paper
crayons

Possible office materials include erasers, paper clips, stickers, and rubber bands.

A youngster sorts the objects and labels her paper with each item. Then she uses tally marks to show how many of each object is in her collection. For additional practice, have her sort a collection of counters or different-colored crayons.

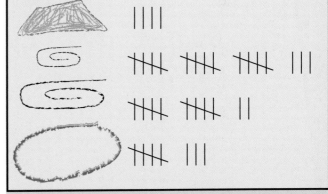

Select a Symbol

Comparing numbers

Materials:
inequality symbol cards: <, >, and =
dominoes
blank paper

A student takes a domino and writes on his paper the sum of the dots. He leaves a space and writes the sum of the dots displayed on a second domino. Then he places the symbol card between the dominoes to make a true statement and writes the symbol on his paper. He continues in this manner with more dominoes as time allows.

Joseph

6 = 6
12 > 2
8 > 3
8 > 5

Cut and Create

Plane shapes

Materials:
square cutouts
blank paper
scissors
glue

A child folds a square to make a triangle shape. She unfolds the triangle and cuts on the line. She continues to fold the triangles to make as many smaller triangles as desired. Then she arranges the triangles to create a picture or design and glues them in place.

Going Fishing

Addition to 18

Materials:
18 fish-shaped crackers in two different colors
   (or fish cutouts in two colors)
net or large scoop
blue paper
blank paper

A student pretends to go fishing and uses the net to catch fish. She unloads the fish onto the blue paper and sorts them by color. Then she writes an addition sentence that describes her catch. She returns the fish to the mixture and continues in this manner as time permits.

Kendra

$7 + 4 = 11$
$5 + 8 = 13$
$4 + 5 = 9$
$8 + 7 = 15$

Spill It!

Fractions

Materials:
tub of counters (two colors)
scoop
blank paper
crayons

A youngster folds his paper to make eight boxes. Then he takes a scoop of counters and sorts them by color. He draws on his paper to show the colors sorted. Next, he uses a matching color crayon to write each fraction for his drawing as shown. After returning the counters to the tub, he continues in this manner for each of the remaining sections on his paper.

$\frac{2}{5}$ $\frac{3}{5}$ $\frac{3}{4}$ $\frac{1}{4}$ $\frac{1}{6}$ $\frac{5}{6}$

Spots and Stripes

Patterns

Materials:
traceable letter cutouts
blank paper
crayons

A youngster traces letters on her paper to spell her name. Then she decorates each letter with spots or stripes to create an extended pattern. For a longer pattern, have her trace both her first and last name.

Cookie Stories

Subtraction to 12

Materials:
12 circle cutouts (cookies)
blank paper
crayons

A student folds her paper to make four boxes as shown. Then she draws one family member, friend, or animal in each box. Next, she places a desired number of cookies by each drawing, takes some away, and writes words and a number sentence to tell what happened to the cookies.

Fact-Filled Flowers

Mixed practice to 10

Materials:
student copies of page 95
6" x 18" construction paper strips (one per student)
scissors
crayons
glue

A student cuts out the patterns and glues the pots to the bottom of her paper strip. Then she solves each math problem and places it above the pot with the same sum. She glues the flowers in place and draws a stem from each flower to its pot.

Money Wheel

Counting coins

Materials:
copy of the coin cards and spinner pattern
    on page 92, prepared as shown
supply of coins
lined paper

For each of three spins on the spinner, a child takes the corresponding coin and draws a coin shape to show where the spinner stopped. He writes the value of each coin in the center, adds the coin values, and writes the sum. He continues in this manner as time permits. For an easier version, provide a copy of the coin cards on page 78 for students to use as a reference.

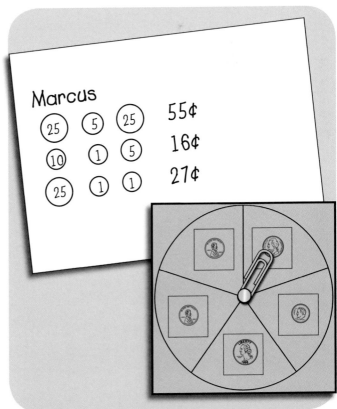

"Eggs-tra" Practice

Fact families

Materials:
plastic eggs, each containing three paper
strips programmed with different
numbers from a chosen fact family
blank paper

A student removes the paper strips from a
selected egg and writes the corresponding addition and subtraction facts on her paper. She
returns the strips to the egg and repeats the
activity with additional eggs.

Nancy

$8 + 7 = 15$
$7 + 8 = 15$
$15 - 8 = 7$
$15 - 7 = 8$

| 8 | 7 | 15 |

"Weigh" to Go!

Weight

Materials:
balance
book that will fit on the balance
various objects, some heavier than
the book and some lighter, that
can fit on the balance

A child selects an object and estimates
whether it is heavier or lighter than the book.
He places it on one side of his work area. He
continues selecting objects until he has sorted
all of them based on whether they are heavier or
lighter than the book. Then he uses the balance
to compare each object with the book to check
his estimates.

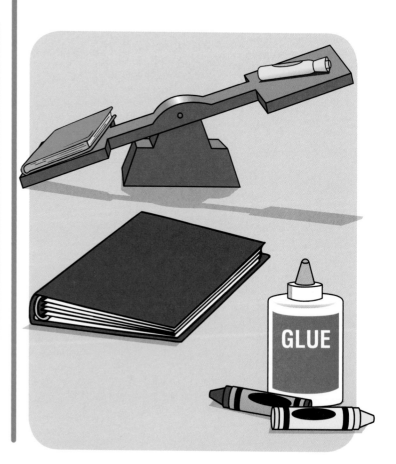

GLUE

Hop, Skip, and Jump

Counting by 2s, 5s, and 10s

Materials:
tagboard copy of page 96, cut apart
hundreds chart
blank paper

A student takes a task card, reads it, and places his kangaroo game piece on the hundreds chart on the starting number. Then he moves the kangaroo as he counts. After he writes the corresponding number pattern on his paper, he continues with the remaining task cards.

Cover Up

Solid figures

Materials:
2 or 3 of each of the following: empty tissue boxes (cubes), party hats (cones), cardboard tubes (cylinders), and shoeboxes (rectangular prisms)
magazines, sale circulars, or newspapers
scissors
glue

A youngster cuts out several pictures of objects representing each solid figure. Then she glues each picture to its corresponding solid figure.

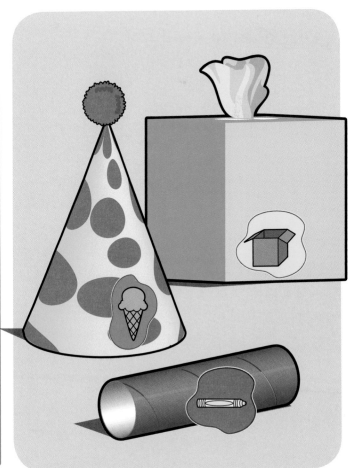

Shake It Up!

Mixed practice

Materials:
container of 18 two-color counters
cup
paper
crayons

A youngster places a handful of counters in the cup. Next, he places his hand atop the cup, shakes the cup, and empties the counters onto a work surface. On his paper, he draws the counters and writes a corresponding addition sentence and subtraction sentence. Then he returns the counters to the container and repeats the activity.

Time for Change

Money

Materials:
paper plates, each labeled with a
    different money amount and four
    stamped coin combinations
supply of coins

A student takes a plate and identifies the money amount in the center. He places a coin atop each stamp while counting to reach the amount in each section. He then removes all the coins and repeats the activity with each of the remaining plates.

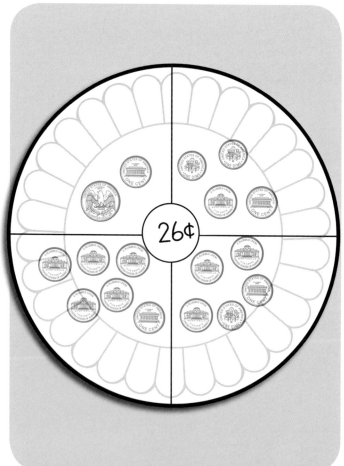

Handy Dandy

Patterns

Materials:
tagboard template of an oversize hand,
  sized to fit a 9" x 11" sheet of paper
construction paper (one per student)
scissors
crayons

A child traces the handprint on a sheet of construction paper and cuts it out. She decides on a pattern and writes the pattern unit on the palm of the hand. She then uses crayons to create five different patterns, one on each of the fingers, that follow the designated pattern unit.

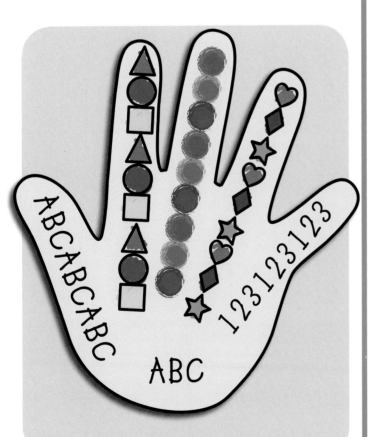

Build It, Count It

Place value

Materials:
cards programmed with two-digit numbers
Unifix cubes
blank paper

A student takes a card and reads the number. She builds the number by counting cubes one at a time. Each time she reaches ten cubes, she snaps them together to form a set of ten. She copies the number on her paper and writes how many tens and how many ones are in the number.

Missy

36 = 3 tens, 6 ones
21 = 2 tens, 1 one
47 = 4 tens, 7 ones

Catch Me if You Can

Mixed practice

Materials:
student copies of page 97 with 4 lightning bugs
  programmed with addition problems and 4
  programmed with subtraction problems
cup
scissors
glue

A student cuts out the lightning bugs from his
sheet and places them in the cup. Next, he gently
tosses the bugs in the air with one hand and
catches a bug or bugs with the other hand. He
determines if the problems on his captured lightning bugs are addition or subtraction problems
and glues them in the corresponding jars on his
sheet. He returns the remaining bugs to the cup
and repeats until all the bugs have been caught.
He then solves the problems.

Don't Be Late!

Time

Materials:
blank cards, each programmed with a clock
  showing a time to the hour
blank paper

A youngster shuffles the clock cards and stacks
them facedown. She draws the top card and
reads the time shown. Then, on her paper, she
writes the digital time that is thirty minutes later
than the time shown on the clock.

Number Squeeze

Skip-counting

Materials:
paper strips (three per student)
3 containers labeled as shown, each containing
  number tiles suitable for counting by the designated number pattern

A child takes a strip of paper, accordion-folds it, and unfolds it. He chooses a tile from the "Count by tens" cup and writes the number in the first section on his strip. He continues the counting pattern in each subsequent section until he reaches the end of the strip. He repeats the activity to count by fives and then to count by twos.

Place Your Order!

Ordinal numbers

Materials:
student copies of page 98
blank paper
scissors
crayons

A student colors and cuts out the food and ordinal number cards. She positions the ordinal number cards in order in a straight line and then places the food cards in any order she chooses. On her paper, she writes sentences telling the order of each food item.

Mix It Up!

Mixed practice

Materials:
a copy of the spinner on page 92, assembled
    as shown, with each section labeled with
    a different number
blank paper

A child spins the spinner two times. By
writing the larger number first and the smaller
number second, she writes and solves an addition problem and a subtraction problem. She
repeats the process until she has written and
solved ten pairs of problems.

Cecilia

1. 9 + 6 = 15   9 − 6 = 3
2. 5 + 4 = 9   5 − 4 = 1
3. 8 + 5 = 13   8 − 5 = 3
4.

Shake It!

Probability

Materials:
sanitized egg carton with each section
    labeled with a number from 1 to 12
pom-pom
blank paper

A student numbers his paper from 1 to 12.
He places a pom-pom in the egg carton; then
he closes the carton and gently shakes it. After
opening the lid, he makes a tally mark on his
paper to show in which space the pom-pom
landed. He continues in this manner until he has
made 20 tally marks. For an added challenge, the
child writes sentences on the back of his paper
about which numbers received the most and
fewest tally marks.

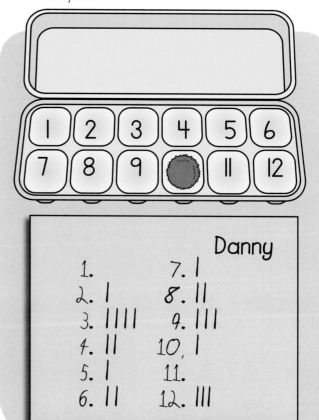

Danny

1.   7. |
2. | 8. ||
3. |||| 9. |||
4. || 10. |
5. | 11.
6. || 12. |||

Happy Birthday!

Place value

Materials:
blank calendar pages (one for each student's birthday month)
crayons

A youngster finds the calendar for his birthday month and writes his name on his birthday. He then circles the numbers in each date that are in the tens place and underlines those that are in the ones place.

September						
Sunday	Monday	Tuesday	Wednesday	Thursday	Friday	Saturday
	1	2	3	4	5	6
7	8	9	⑩	⑪	⑫	⑬
⑭	⑮	⑯	⑰	⑱	⑲	⑳
㉑	㉒	㉓	Selassie ㉔	㉕	㉖	㉗
㉘	㉙	㉚				

Finish It

Number patterns

Materials:
paper strips, each labeled with the beginning of a number pattern and then laminated
wipe-off markers
damp paper towel

A student selects a strip and uses the wipe-off marker to complete the number pattern. She repeats with the remaining strips and then uses the damp paper towel to erase the marker. For an added challenge, the child turns a strip over and writes her own number pattern on the back.

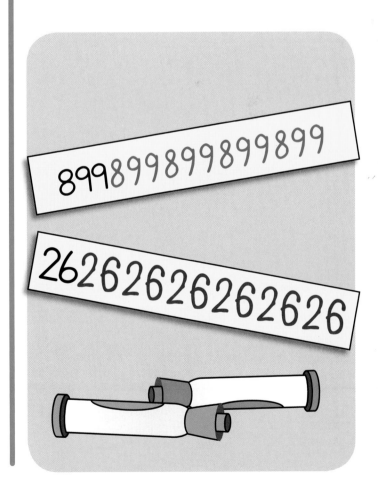

Set 25

Flutter Bugs

Subtraction word problems

Materials:
student copies of page 99
blank paper
scissors
crayons
glue

A student cuts out the word problem and bug cards. He takes a word problem card, glues it to his paper, and uses the bug cards to help him solve the problem. Then he writes the answer next to the card. He continues in this manner with each remaining card, using the back of his paper as needed.

Fishy Fun

Plane shapes

Materials:
student copies of the fish patterns on page 100
pattern blocks
blue construction paper (one per student)
scissors
crayons
glue

A student places pattern blocks on one fish to match its shape. She uses a different geometric design to cover the second fish shape. Then she traces each pattern block and colors the fish to match each design. To complete the activity, she cuts out her fish, glues them to her blue paper, and adds desired details.

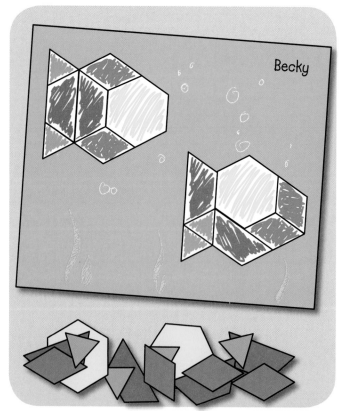

Around the Block

Fact families

Materials:
8 house cutouts (pattern on page 100)
    programmed with the numbers in
    different fact families
blank paper
crayons

A youngster folds a sheet of paper to create eight sections and draws a small house in each section. Then she takes a programmed house, copies the information on one of her houses, and writes the corresponding fact family in that section. She continues with the remaining houses as she moves around the block.

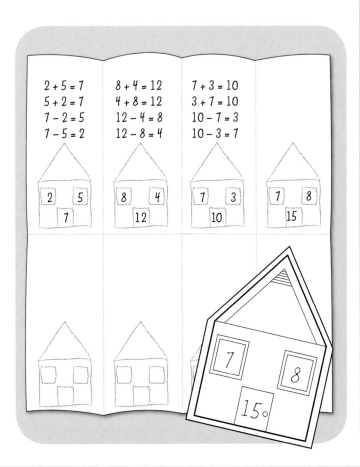

Colorful Counting

Place value

Materials:
1" x 10" paper strips (tens)
1" paper squares (ones)
hundreds board
pom-pom
blank paper
glue

A student tosses the pom-pom on the hundreds board and writes on his paper the number on which the pom-pom lands. After determining how many tens and ones are in the number, he glues the corresponding number of strips and squares on his paper. He continues in this manner as time allows.

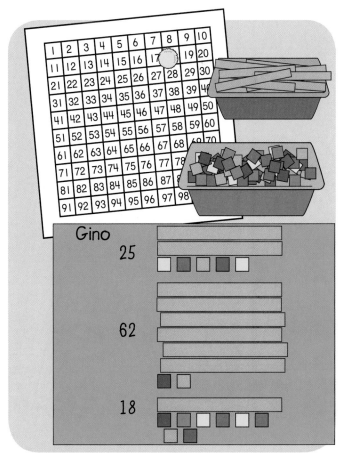

Set 26

How Many Crayons?

Data analysis

Materials:
student copies of page 76, titled as shown
student copies of the recording sheet on page 101
crayons (3 red, 7 green, 3 blue, 5 orange, 1 purple)

A youngster labels the bottom of her graph with the five different crayon colors. She colors one box in the corresponding column for each crayon. Then she uses the completed graph to answer the questions on her recording sheet.

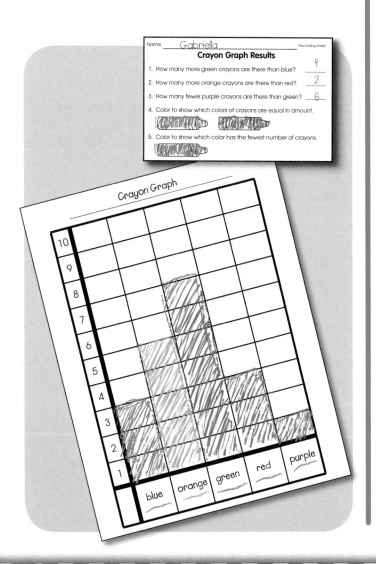

Valuable Names

Addition

Materials:
list of students' names (one per student)

For each name on the list, a student writes the number of letters in the first and last name. Then he uses the two numbers to create addition sentences, as shown. For a more advanced version, have him add the numbers of two full names.

Lynn		
5	7	
Becky Andrews		5 + 7 = 12
5	6	
Diane Badden		5 + 6 = 11
9	5	
Kimberley Bruck		9 + 5 = 14
5	7	
Jenny Chapman		5 + 7 = 12
4	6	
Lynn Drolet		
4	5	
Lori Henry		
4	8	
Thad McLaurin		
3	6	
Max Murphy		
6	6	
Sharon Murphy		
5	6	
Gerri Primak		
4	8	
Zane Williard		

Inchworm Predictions

Linear measurement

Materials:
student copies of the inchworm ruler on page 101
blank paper
scissors
crayons
glue

A youngster colors, cuts out, and glues the inchworm strips together to make a ruler. Next, she writes on her paper an estimate of her shoe length in inches. Then she traces her shoe on her paper, uses her inchworm ruler to measure it, and compares the true length to her prediction.

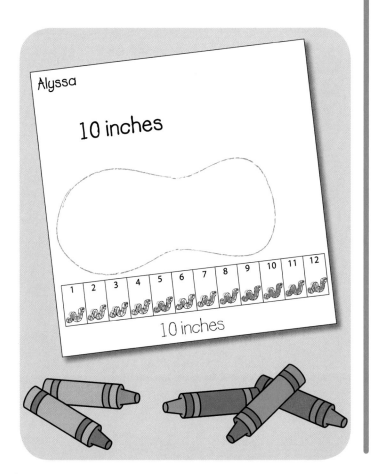

King's Coins

Money

Materials:
copy of the coin cards on page 102, cut apart
student copies of the recording sheet on page 102
coin manipulatives

A student takes a coin card and finds the corresponding manipulatives. He adds the coin values and writes the sum next to the matching letter on his recording sheet. He continues in this manner for each remaining card.

What's for Lunch?

Mixed practice

Materials:
copy of page 103, cut apart
4 paper bags, labeled as shown

To pack four balanced meals, a youngster solves the math problem for each food card and places it in the bag labeled with the answer.

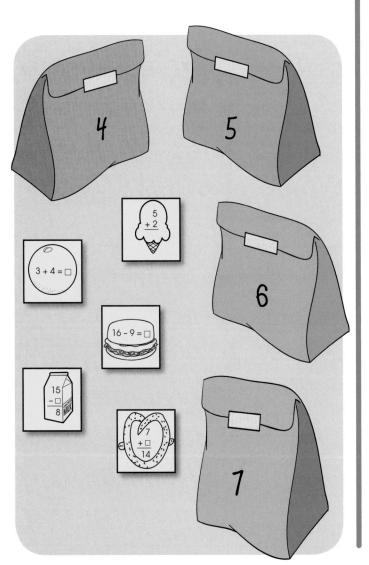

Cube Connections

Place value

Materials:
resealable bags labeled *A* to *E*, each with a desired
    number of Unifix cubes
writing paper

A student labels his paper as shown. He empties the first bag and connects the cubes to make groups of ten. Then he counts the groups of ten and the remaining cubes and records his findings in the corresponding columns on his paper. He continues in this manner with the remaining four bags.

Liam

	Tens	Ones	Number
A.	4	3	43
B.	5	9	59
C.			
D.			
E			

Seasonal Strips

Patterns

Materials:
die
long paper strips (one per student)
crayons

A student thinks of a seasonal item that is easy to draw. Once he has decided on the item, he rolls the die and uses a crayon to draw a corresponding number of the items on his strip. After choosing a second seasonal item, he rolls the die again and repeats the process with that item. Then he continues the pattern to the end of the strip. If time permits, he repeats the activity on the back of his strip.

Family Fun

Counting by 2s, 5s, and 10s

Materials:
blank paper
crayons

A student draws on a sheet of paper each member of her family, making sure to include details to show eyes, fingers, and toes. Then she counts by twos, fives, and tens to write, respectively, how many eyes, fingers, and toes are in her family.

Barbara

6 eyes
30 fingers
30 toes

Crafty Comparisons

Comparing numbers

Materials:
pipe cleaners cut in half
number cards from 0–100
blank paper
tape

A student takes a number card and writes its number on the left side of his paper. Then he takes a different card and writes its number on the right side. He folds a pipe cleaner and tapes the resulting greater than or less than symbol to make a true number statement. He continues in this manner as time permits.

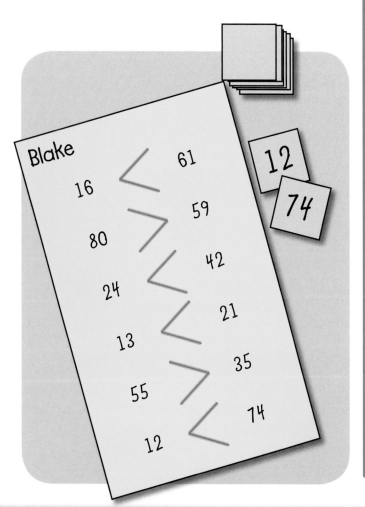

Sticker Stories

Word problems

Materials:
stickers (suggest a maximum amount per student)
blank paper
crayons

A student uses the stickers and crayons to create a word problem scene on his paper. Then he writes the word problem and the corresponding number sentence.

Take a Look!

Plane shapes

Materials:
copy of the shape workmat on page 86
blank paper
crayons

A youngster folds his paper to make six sections. He draws and labels a shape in each section to match the shape workmat. Next, for each shape, he looks around the classroom (or out the window) to identify an object with the same shape; then he draws the object in the corresponding section.

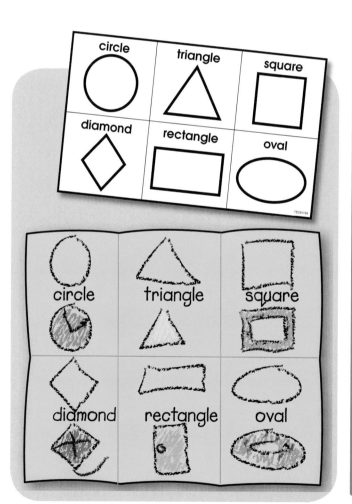

Ant Addends

Addition with three addends

Materials:
die
blank paper

A student folds her paper to create eight sections and draws a three-part ant in each section, as shown. For each ant, she rolls the die three times, writing each number in a different part of the ant. She then adds the three numbers together to find the sum.

In the Cards

Mixed practice

Materials:
deck of playing cards with jacks, kings, and queens removed (jokers and aces remain as zeros and ones)
blank paper

A student shuffles the cards and deals three cards to herself. She stacks the remaining cards facedown. She studies her cards to see if she can create an addition fact. If she can, she writes the fact on her paper and then writes a subtraction fact using the same numbers. If she is unable to create a fact, she draws cards until she can. After writing an addition and a subtraction sentence, she sets the cards aside. She continues in this manner until she has no more cards.

Maria

$8 + 2 = 10$ $10 - 2 = 8$
$5 + 0 = 5$ $5 - 5 = 0$
$7 + 2 = 9$ $9 - 7 = 2$

Pick Two

Place value

Materials:
bag containing number cards from 0 to 9
writing paper

A child removes two cards from the bag. On his paper, he writes the two, two-digit numbers that can be made with the numbers on the cards. Then, beside each two-digit number, he writes how many tens and how many ones are in each number. After he returns the cards to the bag, he draws two more cards to repeat the process. For an added challenge, the child circles the greater number in each set.

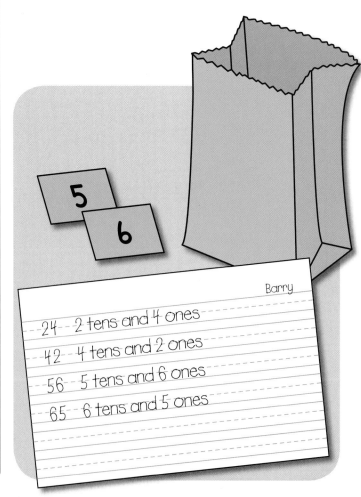

Barry

24   2 tens and 4 ones
42   4 tens and 2 ones
56   5 tens and 6 ones
65   6 tens and 5 ones

Another View

Slides, turns, and flips

Materials:
three different tagboard shapes
three cards labeled as shown
blank paper

A child selects a shape cutout and a card. He traces his shape onto his paper and then traces it three more times, following the chosen direction card. Then he repeats the activity with the remaining two shapes and cards.

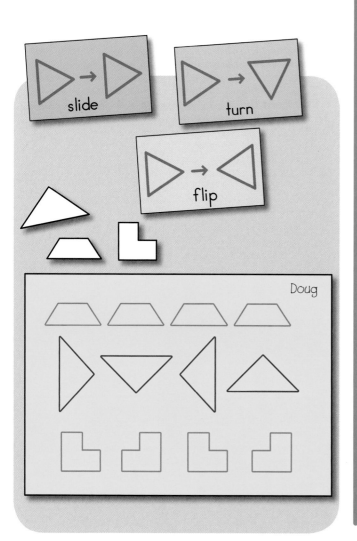

Centimeter Snakes

Linear measurement

Materials:
construction paper copy of page 104, cut apart
writing paper
centimeter ruler

A student measures Snake A with her ruler. On her paper, she writes "Snake A is __ centimeters long" and fills in the measurement. She continues until she has measured and recorded the lengths of all the snakes.

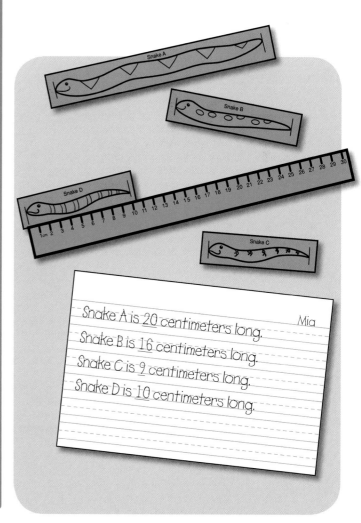

Cute Critters

Two-digit addition

Materials:
animal-shaped paper or die-cuts programmed
    with a math problem
blank paper

A student folds her paper to make eight boxes.
Then she copies and solves a different math
problem in each box.

What Are the Chances?

Probability

Materials:
student copies of page 105
construction paper (one per student)
scissors
glue

A child folds a sheet of construction paper to
create four sections and labels each section as
shown. Next, he cuts apart the cards; reads each
one; and determines if the statement is certain,
likely, unlikely, or impossible. He then glues
each card in the corresponding section of his
paper. For an added challenge, the student writes
an additional event in each section.

Domino Dots

Fact families

Materials:
dominoes
blank paper

A student folds his paper to create four sections. He randomly chooses a domino and draws it at the top of the first section. He writes the two numbers from the domino as an addition problem and solves it. Then he writes the three remaining number sentences in the fact family. He repeats the process for the remaining three boxes.

Monster Machines

Algebra

Materials:
copy of page 106, cut apart
blank paper

A youngster takes a card and copies the chart and the rule on her paper. Then she uses the rule to complete the remainder of the chart. She continues in this manner with the remaining cards.

Three Pizzas, Please!

Fractions

Materials:
copy of page 107, cut apart
3 paper plates labeled as shown
blank paper

A child sets the plates in front of him. He places a pizza topping card in each section of each plate. Then he lists on his paper what fraction of each pizza is made up of each ingredient. For additional practice, he removes the toppings and repeats the activity.

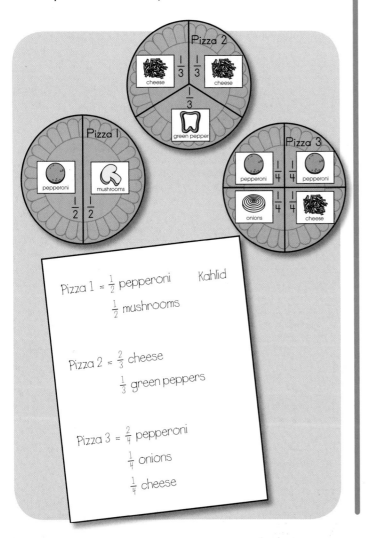

Double-Digit Dice

Numbers to 99

Materials:
die, each side covered and labeled either
    0, 1, 2, 3, 4, or a star
die, each side covered and labeled either
    5, 6, 7, 8, 9, or a star
student copies of a hundreds chart
highlighter

A student rolls the dice and forms a two-digit number with the two rolled numbers. (She may put the numbers in any order she chooses.) If she rolls a star, she may choose any number she wants. Once she makes her number, she uses the highlighter to mark the two-digit number on her hundreds chart. She continues in this manner until she has highlighted a complete row or column.

1	2	3	4	5	6	7	8	9	10
11	12	13	14	15	16	17	18	19	20
21	22	23	24	25	26	27	28	29	30
31	32	33	34	35	36	37	38	39	40
41	42	43	44	45	46	47	48	49	50
51	52	53	54	55	56	57	58	59	60
61	62	63	64	65	66	67	68	69	70
71	72	73	74	75	76	77	78	79	80
81	82	83	84	85	86	87	88	89	90
91	92	93	94	95	96	97	98	99	100

Create a Creature

Solid figures

Materials:
6 solid figures in a bag
list of numbered creature body parts as shown
12" x 18" sheet of construction paper (one per student)
colorful construction paper scraps
scissors
glue

A youngster removes a solid figure from the bag. He counts the flat face(s) and then cuts out the number of eyes to correspond to the number of faces. After setting the figure aside, he selects another one, counts the faces, and cuts out a corresponding number of noses. He repeats the process four more times for mouths, ears, arms, and legs. Then he trims the large sheet of construction paper as desired and glues the body parts in place to create a creature.

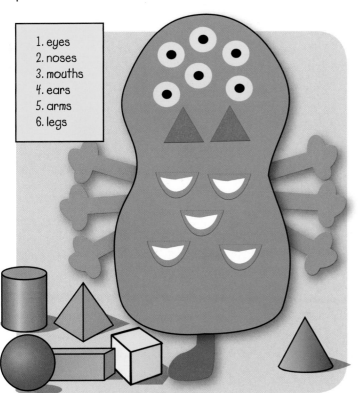

1. eyes
2. noses
3. mouths
4. ears
5. arms
6. legs

Silly Stories

Subtraction word problems

Materials:
copy of page 108, cut apart and sorted
    by number into three containers
writing paper

A student takes one card from each container and then arranges the cards in numerical order. She copies the resulting story problem on her paper and then writes and solves the subtraction problem. If desired, she adds an illustration to the problem. Then she returns the cards to their corresponding containers and repeats the activity to create different word problems.

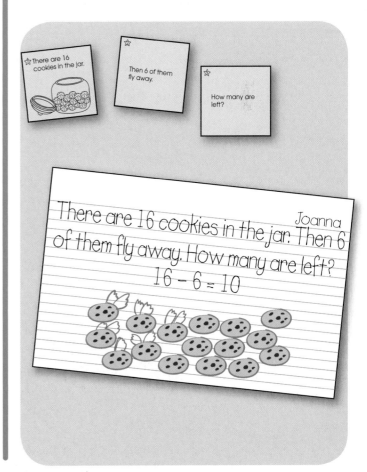

There are 16 cookies in the jar. Then 6 of them fly away. How many are left?
16 − 6 = 10

Roll, Write, and Draw!

Comparing numbers

Materials:
pair of dice
blank paper
crayons

A student rolls the dice and uses the numbers rolled to write a two-digit number on her paper. She rolls again and writes the second number beside the first, leaving a space between them. Then she draws a desired critter, such as a shark or an alligator, between the two numbers so its mouth is opening toward the greater number. She continues in this manner until she has created a predetermined amount of number sentences using each inequality sign.

Take Your Time

Time

Materials:
blank paper

A child folds a sheet of paper into three sections, unfolds it, and titles each column as shown. In the first column, he lists things that take approximately a second to do; in the second column, things that take about a minute to do; and in the third column, things that take close to an hour to do.

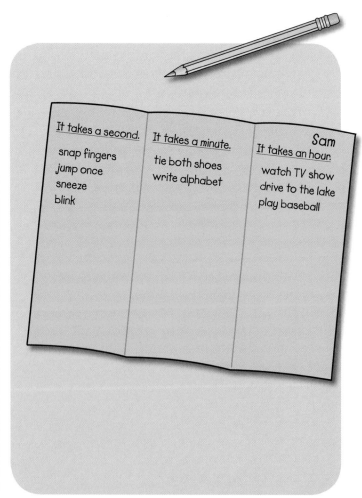

Pick a Stick

Subtraction

Materials:
10 craft sticks numbered in red from 0 to 9
    and placed number-end down in a red cup
 9 craft sticks numbered in blue from 10 to 18
    and placed number-end down in a blue cup
blank paper

    A youngster randomly selects one stick from the blue cup and one stick from the red cup. He arranges the sticks to create a subtraction problem and then copies and solves it on his paper. He replaces the sticks and repeats the activity until he has solved ten problems.

16
8

Ron

18 – 5 = 13
11 – 6 = 5
16 – 8 = 8

Double Scoops!

Problem solving

Materials:
various colors of ice cream scoop cutouts
ice cream cone cutout
sign like the one shown
blank paper
crayons

    A student lays out the ice cream scoops and identifies each flavor. To determine how many different ice cream treats can be made, she combines the ice cream scoops, two at a time, and lists or draws the ingredients for each treat.

Flavors: chocolate
vanilla
strawberry
mint
How many combinations of ice cream treats can be made if each cone has two scoops of ice cream?

Tessa
chocolate, vanilla
chocolate, strawberry
chocolate, mint
mint, vanilla
mint, strawberry
strawberry, vanilla

Set 33

Cube Colors

Graphing

Materials:
student copies of page 76
cards programmed with the sentence starters shown
Unifix cubes (7 red, 3 orange, 7 yellow,
    10 green, and 5 blue)
blank paper

A student sorts the Unifix cubes by color and labels the graph with the matching color words and a title. Next, he colors the columns to match the cubes. Then he copies the sentence starters from the cards onto his paper and completes the sentences by interpreting the graph.

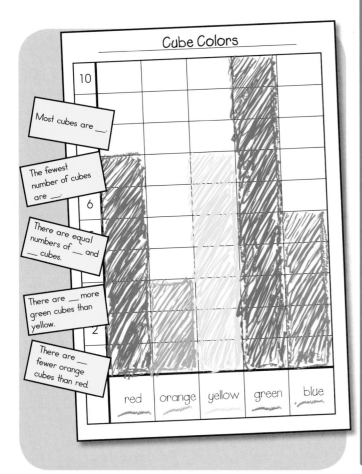

Cube Colors

Most cubes are ___.

The fewest number of cubes are ___.

There are equal numbers of ___ and ___ cubes.

There are ___ more green cubes than yellow.

There are ___ fewer orange cubes than red.

red orange yellow green blue

Fill 'em Up!

Mixed practice

Materials:
pair of dice
12-section recording sheet, similar to the
    one shown (one per student)

A child rolls the dice and chooses whether to add or subtract the two numbers rolled. Then he writes the problem on his recording sheet under the correct answer. He repeats the process until he has written at least one problem in each of the 12 sections.

1	2	3	4	5	6
3 − 2			6 − 2	4 + 1	
7	8	9	10	11	12
4 + 3 5 + 2	3 + 5				6 + 6

Self-Portraits

Linear measurement

Materials:
5 cards, similar to the ones shown
centimeter ruler
construction paper
writing paper
crayons

A student draws a full-page self-portrait on construction paper, being sure to include eyes, a nose, a mouth, and ears. Then she reads the name of a body part from one of the cards, measures that body part on her drawing, and writes on her paper a sentence that includes the measurement to the nearest centimeter. After setting the card aside, she repeats the activity with the remaining cards.

Mix It Up

Place value

Materials:
container of number cards from 0–9
blank paper

A youngster makes a two-column chart and titles the columns as shown. To begin, she removes two cards at random and arranges them to form the largest number possible. Next, she identifies the numbers in the tens and ones places, names the number, and records it in the appropriate column of her chart. Then she rearranges the cards to create the smallest possible number and repeats the activity. She continues with other cards as time allows. For an added challenge, a child chooses three cards and makes three-digit numbers.

Shapely Riddles

Problem solving

Materials:
construction paper copy of page 109, cut apart
blank paper

A student reads card A and looks at the diagram card to determine the answer. After writing the answer on her paper, she continues with the remaining cards.

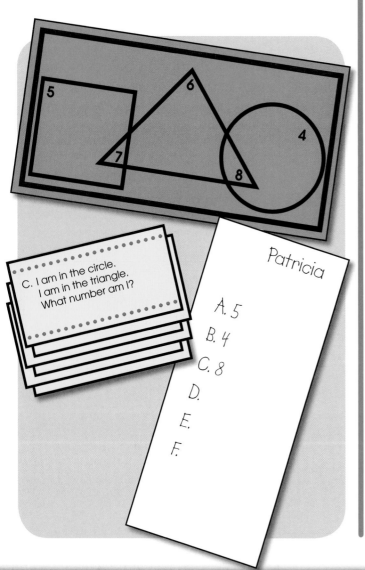

C. I am in the circle.
I am in the triangle.
What number am I?

Patricia

A. 5
B. 4
C. 8
D.
E.
F.

Most Likely?

Probability

Materials:
student copies of the tally chart on page 110, programmed as shown
Unifix cubes in a container (10 blue, 6 red, 6 orange, and 3 yellow)
paper lunch bag
blank paper

A child sorts the cubes by color and labels each row on his chart with a cube color. After counting the cubes of each color, he writes at the bottom of his paper which color he is most likely to pull out of the bag and which color he is least likely to pull out. Next, he puts the cubes in the bag and gives it a shake. He removes a cube without looking and draws a tally mark in the corresponding row on his chart. Then he places the cube back in the bag and repeats the activity nine more times. To complete the activity, he totals the tally marks for each color and checks his prediction.

Recording sheet

Name	Tally Marks	Total
red		
blue		
yellow		
orange		

I am most likely to pull out a(n) _____
I am least likely to pull out a(n) _____

Greg

Recording sheet

	Tally Marks	
red	||	
blue	##H	2
yellow			5
orange	||	1
		2

I am most likely to pull out a(n) __blue cube__
I am least likely to pull out a(n) __yellow cube__

Show That Value!

Money

Materials:
jumbo cutout divided into 8 to 10 sections and
    labeled with different money amounts
beanbag or large pom-pom
coin stampers
ink pad
blank paper

A student folds his paper into six sections
and unfolds it. He places the cutout on the floor
and gently tosses the beanbag onto the cutout.
He announces the money amount in the section
where the beanbag landed. Then he writes the
amount in the first section of his paper and uses
the stampers to show that amount. He repeats
the activity, each time trying to toss the beanbag
onto a different money amount, until he has
filled all six sections of his paper.

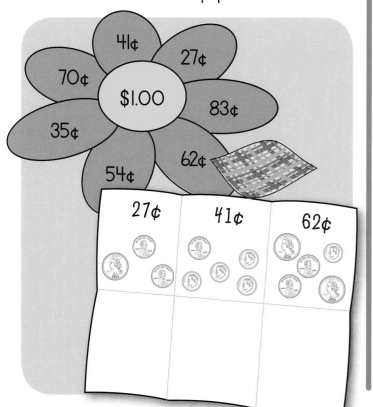

Roll a Rule

Number patterns

Materials:
die
blank paper

A youngster rolls the die to determine the
starting number of the pattern and records the
number on her paper. She rolls the die again to
determine what her addition rule will be. Then
she adds that number to her starting number
and records the sum. She continues to add the
number to each new sum three more times to
create a number pattern. She creates additional
number patterns as time allows.

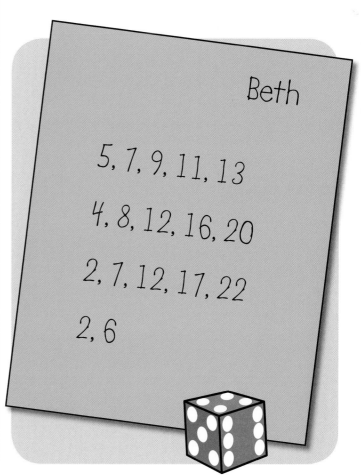

Set 35

Off the Charts!

Mixed practice

Materials:
student copies of the recording sheet on page 110
blank cards, each programmed with
   a different number greater than 5

A youngster stacks the cards facedown. He takes a card and writes the number on the recording sheet. Then he completes the row by using the operation shown at the top of each column. He repeats the process for the remaining four rows. For an added challenge, the child circles the largest number in each row and underlines the smallest number in each row.

Name ___Peter___ Recording sheet

OFF the Charts!

Number	+ 5	– 4	– 6	+ 7
7	12	3	1	14
9	14	5	3	16
6	11	2	0	13

In the Cards

Probability

Materials:
copy of the tally chart on page 110, programmed as
   shown (one per student)
deck of playing cards

A student looks through the deck of cards, noticing how many aces and face cards are in the deck. Then he completes the statements at the bottom of his chart. Next, he shuffles the cards and randomly removes ten cards, placing them facedown. As he turns over each card, he draws a tally mark in the appropriate row of his chart. Then he totals the tally marks for each card type and checks his prediction.

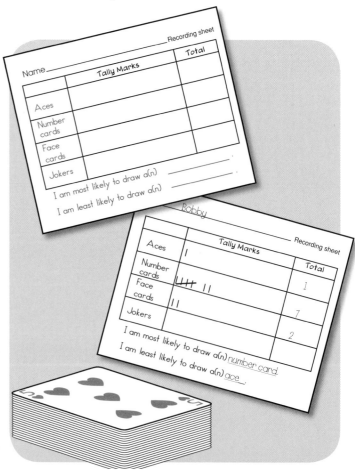

Name _____ Recording sheet

	Tally Marks	Total
Aces		
Number cards		
Face cards		
Jokers		

I am most likely to draw a(n) _____
I am least likely to draw a(n) _____

Bobby Recording sheet

	Tally Marks	Total
Aces	I	1
Number cards	LHT II	7
Face cards	II	2
Jokers		

I am most likely to draw a(n) _number card_.
I am least likely to draw a(n) _ace_.

Butterflies Flutter

Fact families

Materials:
tagboard butterfly template
blank cards, each programmed with the three
    numbers of a fact family
colorful construction paper
scissors
crayons

A youngster traces the butterfly template onto a sheet of construction paper and cuts the tracing out. She randomly selects a fact family card and writes the three numbers on the body of the butterfly. On each wing, she writes a different fact family number sentence. Then she decorates her butterfly as time allows.

Blown Away

Linear measurement

Materials:
inch ruler
yardstick
pom-pom
piece of masking tape on the floor marking
    a starting line
roll of masking tape
blank paper

A student places the pom-pom on the starting line and estimates how many inches she can blow the pom-pom in one breath. After recording her estimate, she kneels behind the pom-pom and blows once. Next, she uses tape to mark the place where the pom-pom stopped. Then she uses a ruler or yardstick to measure the distance the pom-pom moved, records the measurement, and compares it to her estimate.

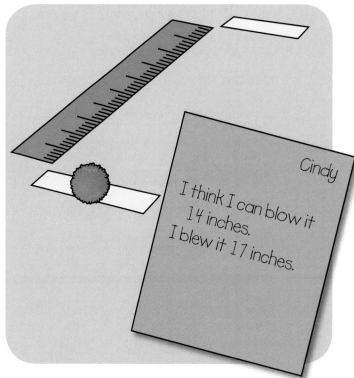

That's Puzzling!

Numbers to 100

Materials:
several copies of a blank hundreds board that has
   been labeled with some numbers,
   laminated, and cut into irregular pieces
wipe-off marker
damp paper towel

A student selects a section of a hundreds board and fills in the missing numbers. Then he uses the paper towel to clean the board before choosing another board to complete. If desired, place a completed hundreds board at the center for students to use as a reference.

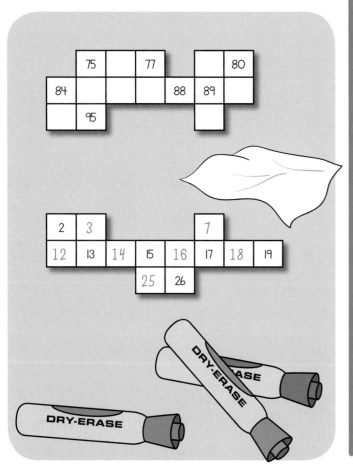

Balance It Out

Weight

Materials:
small classroom objects that can fit on one side of a
   balance
balance
supply of Unifix cubes
blank paper

A youngster folds her paper to make three columns and titles each column as shown. She holds one of the objects and estimates how many Unifix cubes it will take to balance it. She writes her estimate in the corresponding column. She places the item on one side of the balance and the cubes on the other. She adds or takes away cubes until she balances the object. Then she records her measurement in the corresponding column. She continues until she has estimated and measured each item.

Object	Estimate	Measure
pencil	about 10 cubes	3 cubes
box of crayons	about 15 cubes	25 cubes
ruler	about 8 cubes	

Roll and Flip

Adding three addends

Materials:
three dice
16 die-cut shapes, each programmed with
   a different number from 3–18

A child lays the shapes in order, number-side up, on a work surface. He rolls the three dice and adds the numbers. Then he finds the numbered shape that matches the sum and turns it over. He continues rolling, adding, and matching numbers until he has turned over all the shapes. If he rolls a sum that matches a shape he has already turned over, he rolls again.

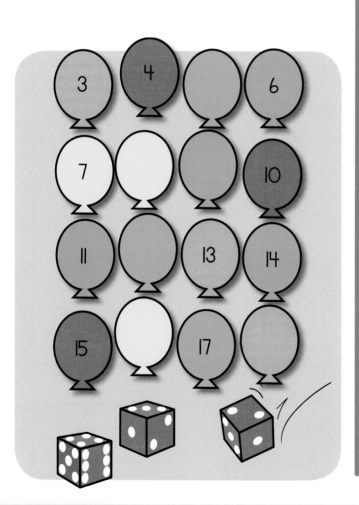

Beanbag Toss

Problem solving

Materials:
large copy of the problem and targets shown
blank paper

A student reads the problem and writes all the possibilities on her paper. For more practice, the child assigns the targets three different numbers and writes those possible scores on the back of her paper.

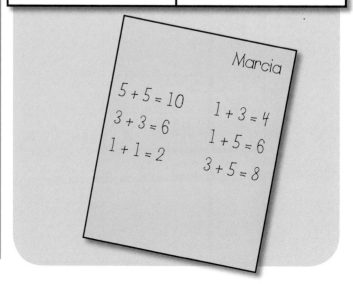

Problem	Targets
If you throw two beanbags and they both hit targets, what scores could you have? Find all of the possibilities.	

Marcia

5 + 5 = 10
3 + 3 = 6
1 + 1 = 2

1 + 3 = 4
1 + 5 = 6
3 + 5 = 8

10					
9					
8					
7					
6					
5					
4					
3					
2					
1					

Note to the teacher: Use with "Bean Bonanza" on page 5, "Color Towers" on page 11, "Goody Goody Gumballs" on page 27, "Take a Spin!" on page 35, "How Many Crayons?" on page 54, and "Cube Colors" on page 68.

TEC61154

Fly and Word Cards

Use with "That Pesky Fly!" on page 7.

| on | above | next to | below |

TEC61154

Coin Cards

Use with "A Valuable Collection" on page 24 and "Money Wheel" on page 43.

Super Simple Independent Practice: Math • ©The Mailbox® Books • TEC61154

Cookie Cards
Use with "Batch of Cookies" on page 13.

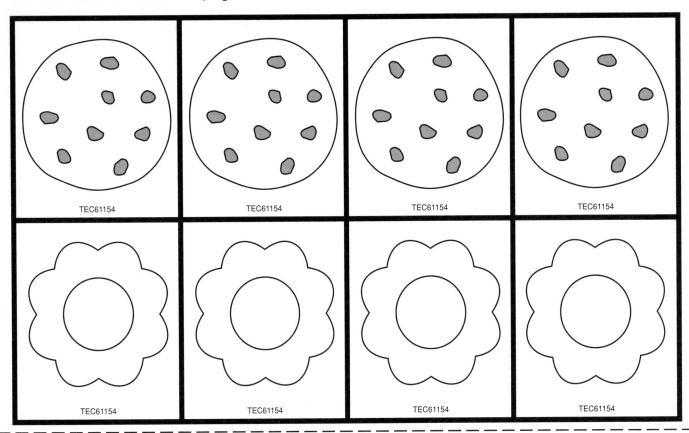

TEC61154   TEC61154   TEC61154   TEC61154

TEC61154   TEC61154   TEC61154   TEC61154

Name_____

My crazy face has:

_____ circles

_____ squares

_____ triangles

_____ rectangles

Super Simple Independent Practice: Math • ©The Mailbox® Books • TEC61154

Note to the teacher: Use with "Crazy Face" on page 14.

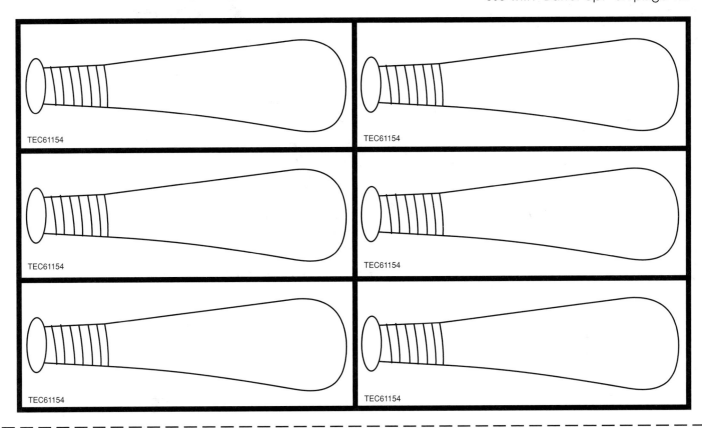

Name _____ Recording Sheet

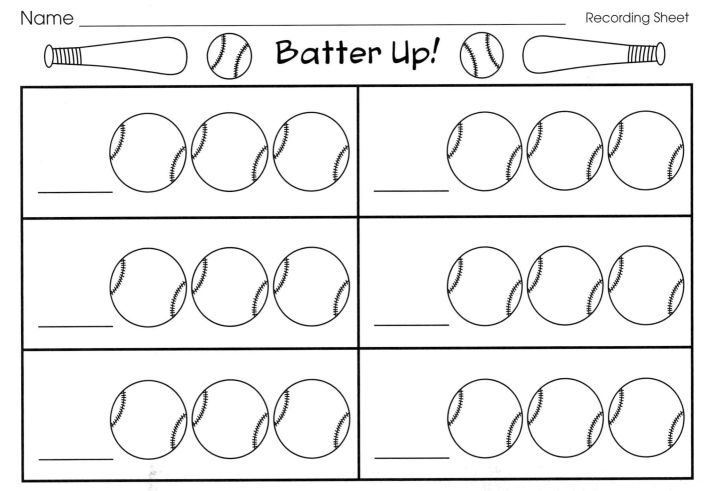

Name

Super Simple Independent Practice: Math • ©The Mailbox® Books • TEC61154

Note to the teacher: Use with "Flower Power" on page 16.

Fill It In

1	2	3	4		6			9	
11				15	16		18		20
		23				27	28		
	32		34	35		37		39	40
41			44	45	46				50

Super Simple Independent Practice: Math • ©The Mailbox® Books • TEC61154

Fill It In

1	2	3	4		6			9	
11				15	16		18		20
		23				27	28		
	32		34	35		37		39	40
41			44	45	46				50

Super Simple Independent Practice: Math • ©The Mailbox® Books • TEC61154

Note to the teacher: Use with "Fill It In" on page 19.

Lily Pad and Frog Cards
Use with "Leaping Lily Pads!" on page 21.

TEC61154

TEC61154

TEC61154

TEC61154

TEC61154

TEC61154

TEC61154

TEC61154

TEC61154

TEC61154

TEC61154

TEC61154

TEC61154

TEC61154

5 pigs.
2 more pigs.
How many pigs are there in all?

TEC61154

6 pigs.
4 more pigs.
How many pigs are there in all?

TEC61154

4 pigs.
3 more pigs.
How many pigs are there in all?

TEC61154

5 pigs.
5 more pigs.
How many pigs are there in all?

TEC61154

7 pigs.
1 more pig.
How many pigs are there in all?

TEC61154

3 pigs.
6 more pigs.
How many pigs are there in all?

TEC61154

4 pigs.
2 more pigs.
How many pigs are there in all?

TEC61154

2 pigs.
3 more pigs.
How many pigs are there in all?

TEC61154

Shape Workmat
Use with "Geometric Rainbow" on page 24 and "Take a Look!" on page 59.

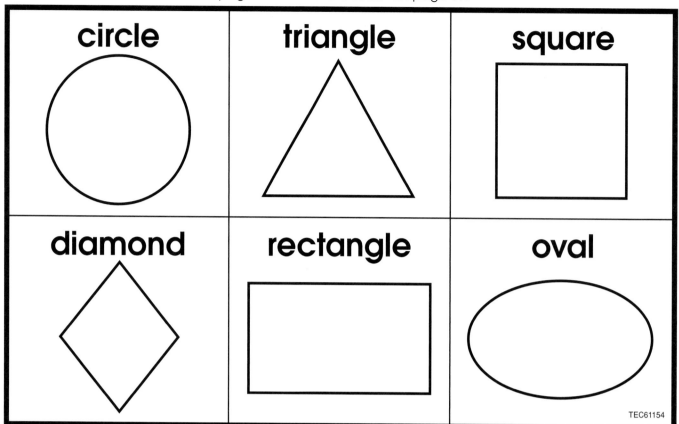

circle

triangle

square

diamond

rectangle

oval

TEC61154

Sunflower Workmat
Use with "Flower Seeds" on page 29.

TEC61154

Super Simple Independent Practice: Math • ©The Mailbox® Books • TEC61154

Big and Bitty Bugs

Color the tallest bug blue.
Color the longest bug yellow.

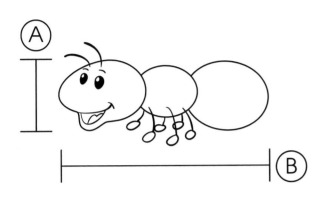

Ⓐ Ⓑ

Ⓒ

Ⓓ

Ⓔ

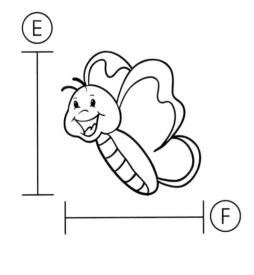

Ⓕ

Ⓗ

Ⓖ

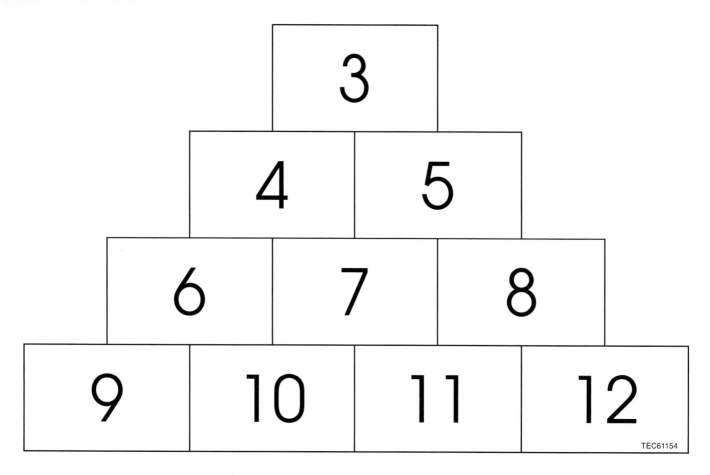

Note to the teacher: Use the pyramid workmat with "Build a Pyramid" on page 26.

Name_____ Recording Sheet

First Grade

‾ ‾ ‾ ‾ ‾ ‾ ‾ ‾ ‾ ‾ ‾ ‾ ‾ ‾ ‾

A. Color the **2nd** letter orange.

B. Color the **7th** letter yellow.

C. Color the **1st** letter red.

D. Color the **8th** letter blue.

E. Color the **3rd** letter yellow.

F. Color the **5th** letter brown.

G. Color the **9th** letter purple.

H. Color the **4th** letter green.

I. Color the **10th** letter black.

J. Color the **6th** letter red.

Super Simple Independent Practice: Math • ©The Mailbox® Books • TEC61154

88   **Note to the teacher:** Use the recording sheet with "A First-Grade Lineup!" on page 27.

Note to the teacher: Use with "Goody Goody Gumballs" on page 27.

89

TEC61154	TEC61154	TEC61154	TEC61154
TEC61154	TEC61154	TEC61154	TEC61154
36 TEC61154	**52** TEC61154	**79** TEC61154	**100** TEC61154
18 TEC61154	**47** TEC61154	**65** TEC61154	**84** TEC61154

Finish the Story

_____ fish swim. Then _____ more fish swim.

How many fish swim in all?

_____ + _____ = _____ fish

_____ frogs sit. Then _____ more frogs sit.

How many frogs sit in all?

_____ + _____ = _____ frogs

_____ ducks swim. Then _____ more ducks swim.

How many ducks swim in all?

_____ + _____ = _____ ducks

_____ dragonflies fly. Then _____ more fly.

How many dragonflies fly in all?

_____ + _____ = _____ dragonflies

Note to the teacher: Use with "Finish the Story" on page 34.

91

Spinner

Use with "Take a Spin!" on page 35, "Money Wheel" on page 43, and "Mix It Up!" on page 50.

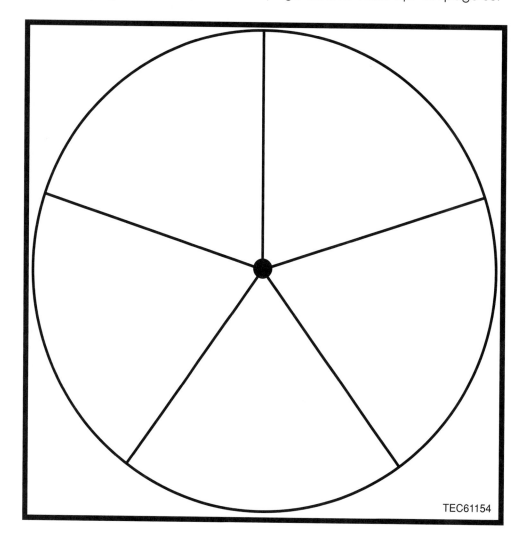

TEC61154

Pet Cards

Use with "Take a Spin!" on page 35.

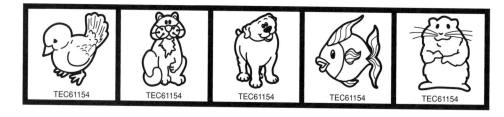

TEC61154   TEC61154   TEC61154   TEC61154   TEC61154

Coin Cards

Use with "Money Wheel" on page 43.

TEC61154   TEC61154   TEC61154   TEC61154   TEC61154

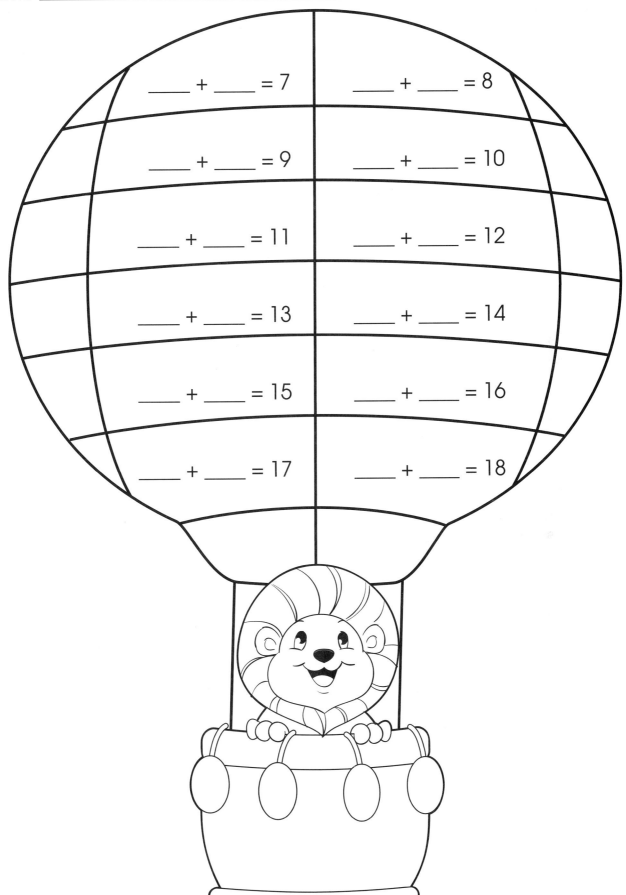

___ + ___ = 7   ___ + ___ = 8

___ + ___ = 9   ___ + ___ = 10

___ + ___ = 11   ___ + ___ = 12

___ + ___ = 13   ___ + ___ = 14

___ + ___ = 15   ___ + ___ = 16

___ + ___ = 17   ___ + ___ = 18

Number and Arrow Wheel Patterns
Use with "What a Wheel!" on page 39.

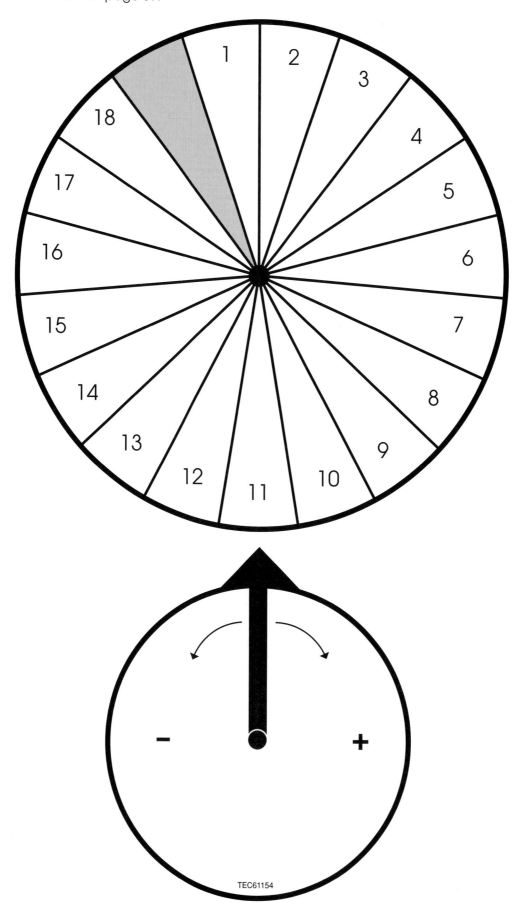

TEC61154

Super Simple Independent Practice: Math • ©The Mailbox® Books • TEC61154

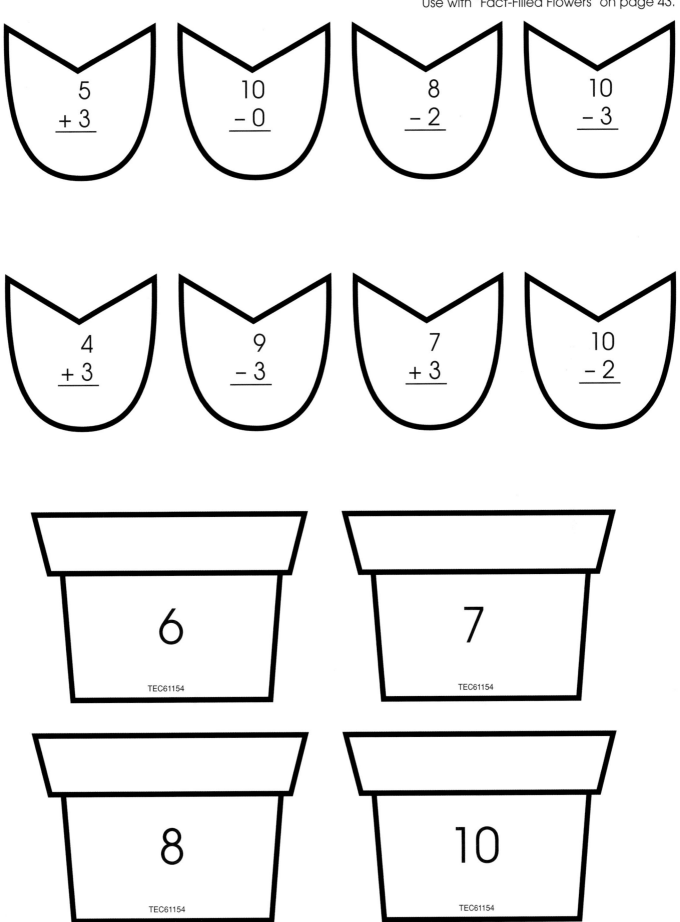

5
+ 3

10
− 0

8
− 2

10
− 3

4
+ 3

9
− 3

7
+ 3

10
− 2

6

7

TEC61154

TEC61154

8

10

TEC61154

TEC61154

Task Cards and Game Pieces

Use with "Hop, Skip, and Jump" on page 45.

A. Go from 5 to 40.
Count by fives.
Write the numbers.

TEC61154

B. Go from 30 to 90.
Count by tens.
Write the numbers.

TEC61154

C. Go from 20 to 50.
Count by twos.
Write the numbers.

TEC61154

D. Go from 75 to 100.
Count by fives.
Write the numbers.

TEC61154

E. Go from 50 to 100.
Count by tens.
Write the numbers.

TEC61154

F. Go from 50 to 80.
Count by twos.
Write the numbers.

TEC61154

G. Go from 10 to 50.
Count by fives.
Write the numbers.

TEC61154

TEC61154

Mixed practice

Catch Me if You Can

Addition

	= ___
	= ___
	= ___

Subtraction

	= ___
	= ___
	= ___

Super Simple Independent Practice: Math • ©The Mailbox® Books • TEC61154

Note to the teacher: Use with "Catch Me if You Can" on page 48.

97

Food and Ordinal Number Cards

Use with "Place Your Order!" on page 49.

fries TEC61154	cake TEC61154	5th fifth TEC61154	10th tenth TEC61154
salad TEC61154	ice cream TEC61154	4th fourth TEC61154	9th ninth TEC61154
pizza TEC61154	fruit TEC61154	3rd third TEC61154	8th eighth TEC61154
hamburger TEC61154	taco TEC61154	2nd second TEC61154	7th seventh TEC61154
hot dog TEC61154	pasta TEC61154	1st first TEC61154	6th sixth TEC61154

3 bugs.
2 fly away.
How many bugs
are left?

TEC61154

6 bugs.
3 fly away.
How many bugs
are left?

TEC61154

10 bugs.
8 fly away.
How many bugs
are left?

TEC61154

7 bugs.
2 fly away.
How many bugs
are left?

TEC61154

2 bugs.
0 fly away.
How many bugs
are left?

TEC61154

5 bugs.
4 fly away.
How many bugs
are left?

TEC61154

8 bugs.
4 fly away.
How many bugs
are left?

TEC61154

9 bugs.
5 fly away.
How many bugs
are left?

TEC61154

TEC61154

Fish Patterns

Use with "Fishy Fun" on page 52.

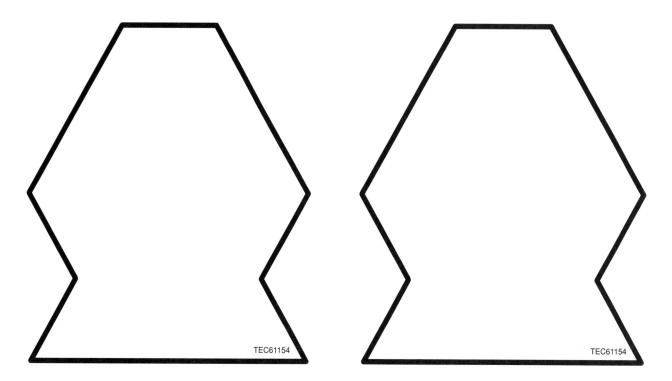

TEC61154 TEC61154

House Pattern

Use with "Around the Block" on page 53.

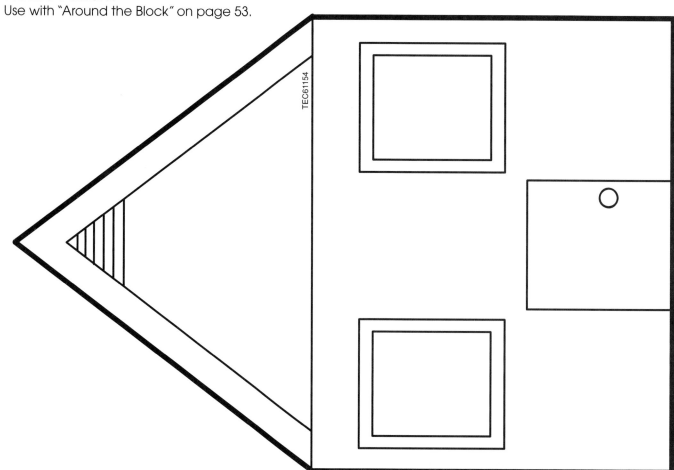

TEC61154

Super Simple Independent Practice: Math • ©The Mailbox® Books • TEC61154

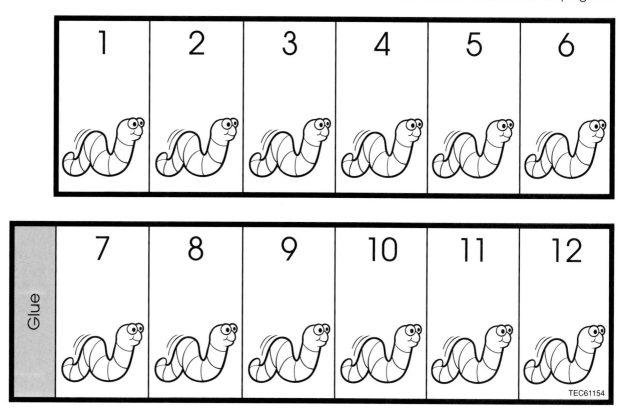

TEC61154

Name_____

Crayon Graph Results

1. How many more green crayons are there than blue? _____

2. How many more orange crayons are there than red? _____

3. How many fewer purple crayons are there than green? _____

4. Color to show which colors of crayons are equal in amount.

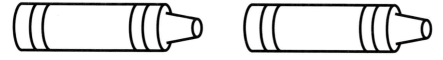

5. Color to show which color has the fewest number of crayons.

Super Simple Independent Practice: Math • ©The Mailbox® Books • TEC61154

Note to the teacher: Use with "How Many Crayons?" on page 54.

101

Coin Sets

Use with "King's Coins" on page 55.

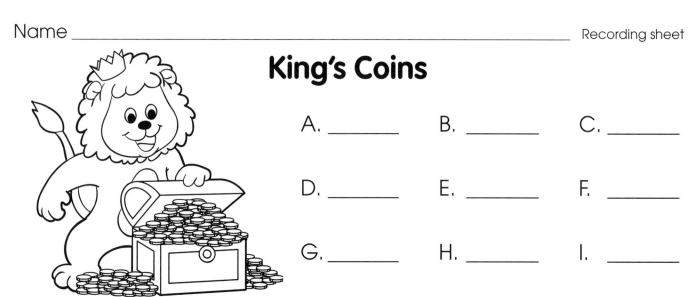

Name _____ Recording sheet

King's Coins

A. _____   B. _____   C. _____

D. _____   E. _____   F. _____

G. _____   H. _____   I. _____

Super Simple Independent Practice: Math • ©The Mailbox® Books • TEC61154

Note to the teacher: Use with "King's Coins" on page 55.

Use with "What's for Lunch?" on page 56.

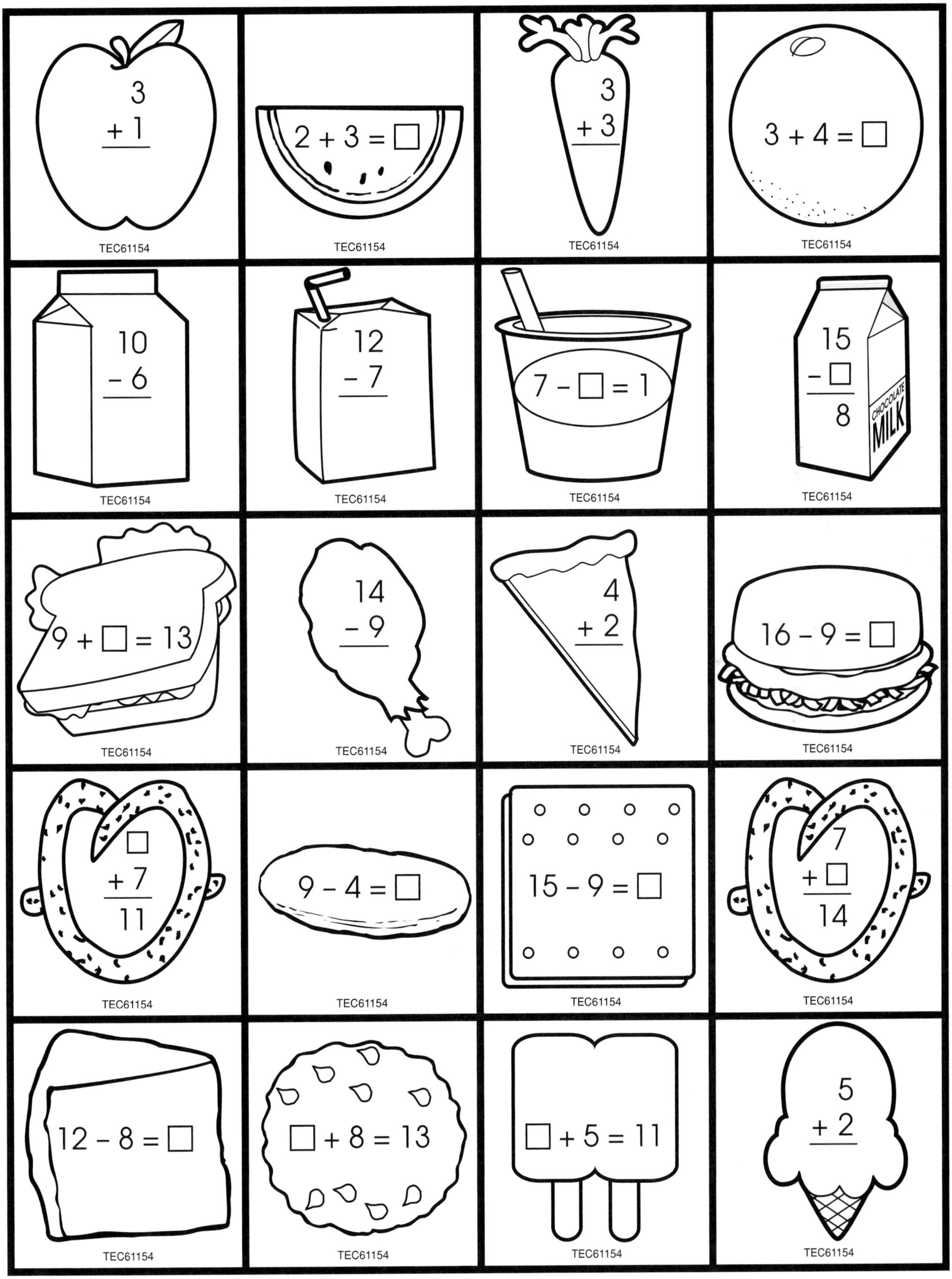
3 + 1
TEC61154
2 + 3 = □
TEC61154
3 + 3
TEC61154
3 + 4 = □
TEC61154
10 − 6
TEC61154
12 − 7
TEC61154
7 − □ = 1
TEC61154
15 − □ = 8
CHOCOLATE MILK
TEC61154
9 + □ = 13
TEC61154
14 − 9
TEC61154
4 + 2
TEC61154
16 − 9 = □
TEC61154
□ + 7 = 11
TEC61154
9 − 4 = □
TEC61154
15 − 9 = □
TEC61154
7 + □ = 14
TEC61154
12 − 8 = □
TEC61154
□ + 8 = 13
TEC61154
□ + 5 = 11
TEC61154
5 + 2
TEC61154

Snake Strips

Use with "Centimeter Snakes" on page 61.

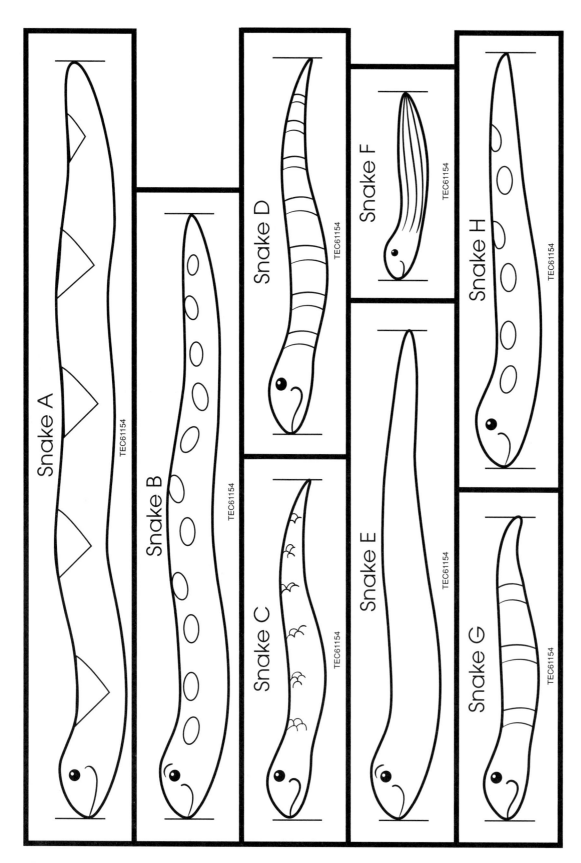

Snake A

Snake B

Snake C

Snake D

Snake E

Snake F

Snake G

Snake H

TEC61154

I will sleep tonight. TEC61154

I will color today. TEC61154

I will climb a mountain today. TEC61154

I will meet a talking bear. TEC61154

I will talk today. TEC61154

I will read today. TEC61154

I will see a whale today. TEC61154

I will ride a magic carpet. TEC61154

I will breathe today. TEC61154

I will play today. TEC61154

I will go scuba diving today. TEC61154

I will meet an alien. TEC61154

I will eat today. TEC61154

I will laugh today. TEC61154

I will ride a plane today. TEC61154

I will graduate from high school today. TEC61154

Monster Cards

Use with "Monster Machines" on page 63.

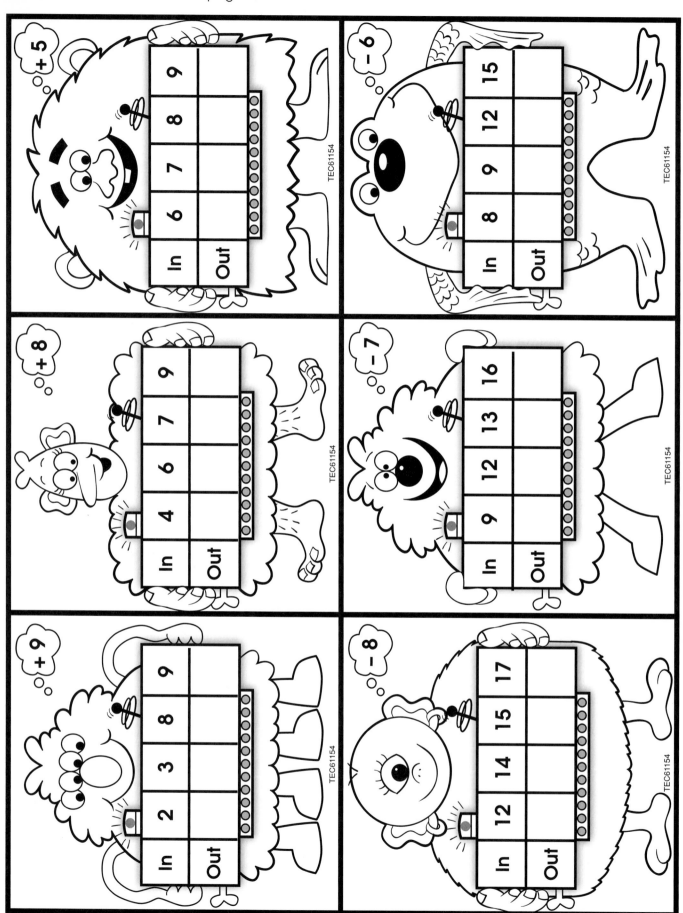

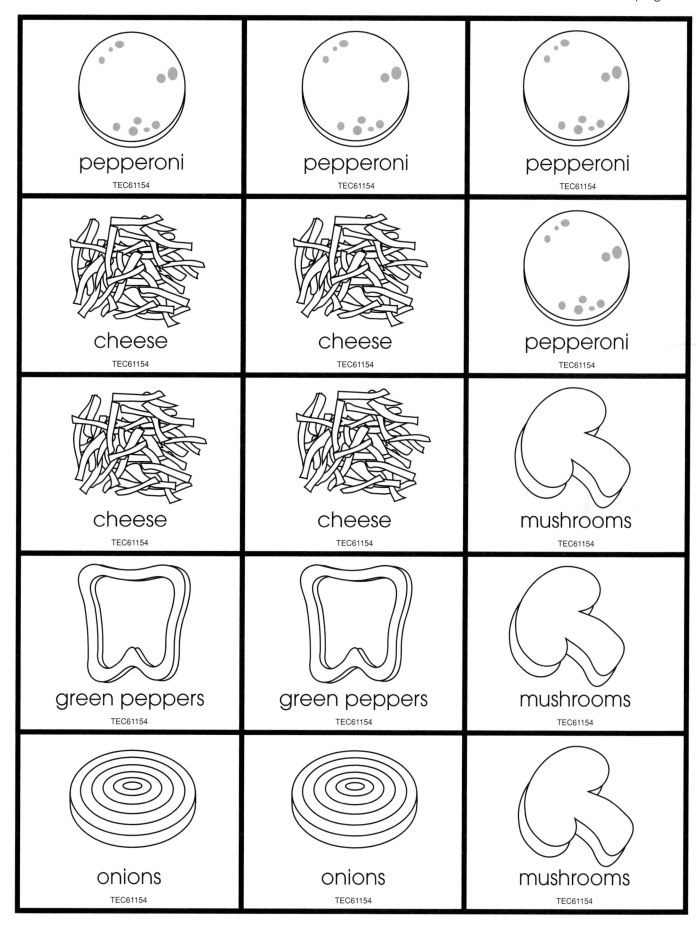

pepperoni
TEC61154

pepperoni
TEC61154

pepperoni
TEC61154

cheese
TEC61154

cheese
TEC61154

pepperoni
TEC61154

cheese
TEC61154

cheese
TEC61154

mushrooms
TEC61154

green peppers
TEC61154

green peppers
TEC61154

mushrooms
TEC61154

onions
TEC61154

onions
TEC61154

mushrooms
TEC61154

Story Cards

Use with "Silly Stories" on page 65.

☆1 There are 12 bugs on the leaf. TEC61154	☆2 Then 2 of them fly away. TEC61154	☆3 How many are left? TEC61154
☆1 There are 16 cookies in the jar. TEC61154	☆2 A little boy takes 5 of them away. TEC61154	☆3 How many are left? TEC61154
☆1 There are 14 cows in the barn. TEC61154	☆2 Then 7 of them roll away. TEC61154	☆3 How many are left? TEC61154
☆1 There are 18 shells on the beach. TEC61154	☆2 A funny clown picks up 8 of them. TEC61154	☆3 How many are left? TEC61154
☆1 There are 15 kites in the sky. TEC61154	☆2 Then 6 of them fly away. TEC61154	☆3 How many are left? TEC61154

Super Simple Independent Practice: Math • ©The Mailbox® Books • TEC61154

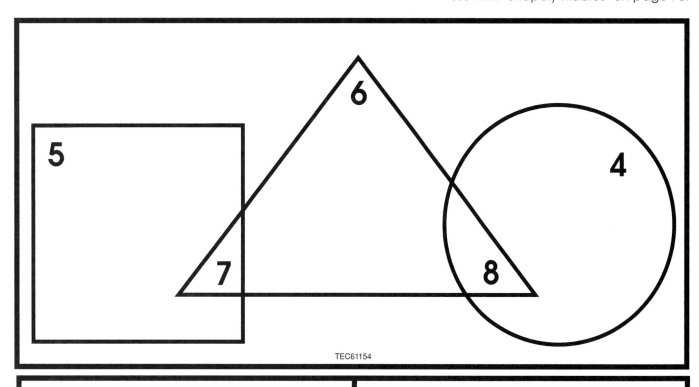

TEC61154

A. I am in the square.
   I am not in the triangle.
   What number am I?

TEC61154

B. I am in the circle.
   I am not in the triangle.
   What number am I?

TEC61154

C. I am in the circle.
   I am in the triangle.
   What number am I?

TEC61154

D. I am in the triangle.
   I am not in the square.
   I am not in the circle.
   What number am I?

TEC61154

E. I am in the square.
   I am in the triangle.
   What number am I?

TEC61154

F. We are in the triangle.
   We are not in the circle.
   What numbers are we?

TEC61154

Name _____

	Tally Marks	Total

Super Simple Independent Practice: Math • ©The Mailbox® Books • TEC61154

Note to the teacher: Use with "Most Likely?" on page 70 and "In the Cards" on page 72.

Name _____ Recording sheet

OFF the Charts!

Number	+ 5	− 4	− 6	+ 7

Super Simple Independent Practice: Math • ©The Mailbox® Books • TEC61154

 Note to the teacher: Use with "Off the Charts!" on page 72.

Skills Index

Data Analysis

bar graph, 5, 11, 18, 27, 35
collecting, recording, and
   interpreting data, 20, 54, 68
probability, 21, 50, 62, 70, 72
tally marks, 39

Geometry

plane shapes
   classifying, 22, 32
   identification, 14, 24, 28, 37, 59
   making new shapes, 40, 52
   modeling, 19
   slides, turns, flips, 61
positional words, 7, 10
solid figures
   identification, 45
   faces, 65

Measurement

nonstandard linear measurement
   comparing length, 15
   measuring, 25, 33, 38, 55, 69
nonstandard weight, 44, 74
standard measurement
   centimeters, 61
   inches, 73

time
   calendar, 9
   elapsed, 48
   to the hour, 29
   understanding of hour, minute,
     and second, 66

Number & Operations

addition
   combinations to 10, 36
   commutative property, 25
   doubles, 22
   equivalent sums, 7, 26
   modeling, 12, 16
   sums to 18,   30, 38, 41
   three addends, 59, 75
   two-digit, 62
   word problems, 23, 34
   writing number sentences, 8, 10,
     15, 18, 54
comparing numbers, 6, 31, 40, 58, 66
count and read numbers to 100,   31
counting, 4, 5
estimation, 13
even and odd numbers, 36
fact families, 44, 53, 63, 73